ENIGMA
CRACK THE CODE

Dr Gareth Moore (B.Sc (Hons) M.Phil Ph.D) is the internationally best-selling author of a wide range of brain-training and puzzle books for both children and adults, including *Anti-stress Puzzles*, *Ultimate Dot to Dot*, *Brain Games for Clever Kids*, *Lateral Logic* and *Extreme Mazes*.

His books have sold over a million copies in the UK alone, and have been published in 29 different languages. He is also the creator of online brain-training site BrainedUp.com, and runs the daily puzzle site PuzzleMix.com.

ENIGMA
CRACK THE CODE

PUZZLES, CODES AND
CHALLENGING CONUNDRUMS
TO TEST YOUR WITS AND
SHARPEN YOUR BRAIN

D R
G A R E T H
M O O R E

Michael O'Mara Books Limited

First published in Great Britain in 2018 by
Michael O'Mara Books Limited
9 Lion Yard
Tremadoc Road
London SW4 7NQ

A CIP catalogue record for this book is available from the
British Library.

Papers used by Michael O'Mara Books Limited are natural,
recyclable products made from wood grown in sustainable forests.
The manufacturing processes conform to the environmental
regulations of the country of origin.

ISBN: 978-1-78243-904-2 in paperback print format

1 2 3 4 5 6 7 8 9 10

www.mombooks.com
www.drgarethmoore.com

Designed and typeset by Gareth Moore
Cover design by Claire Cater
Printed and bound by CPI Group (UK) Ltd, Croydon CR0 4YY

Contents

For my family

Introduction

Welcome to *Enigma: Crack the Code*.

This is no ordinary puzzle book, so if you find a word search a challenge, and a crossword is beyond all hope, then put the book back down right now. You haven't got a chance.

But if you enjoy puzzles, and are up for a challenge, then you certainly have a treat in store! This book is packed from cover to cover with all kinds of enigma, and – with very few exceptions – no two of them are quite the same. Oh, and there are no crosswords or ordinary word searches *anywhere* in this book.

1. Begin Your Challenge

Where to start? Well, chapter 1 is a pretty good place. The book is designed to get harder as you progress, on a chapter-by-chapter basis.

Unlike most puzzle books, however, it's not always the actual difficulty of the puzzle itself that gets harder, but rather how *obscure* the instructions are. In this book, you are not always told what to do – in fact, most of the time it's up to *you* to work out what to do.

How does this work? It's pretty simple. If I think you will be able to solve a puzzle without me telling you exactly what to do, then I'll keep the instructions brief. But if I think you will most likely need some help, I'll give you some more specific instructions.

You are never expected to be psychic, so in other words every puzzle is designed to be fair, but experience with word puzzles will definitely help you – which brings us back to starting at the beginning.

In chapter 1, the instructions are much more explicit and are more likely to tell you exactly what you are supposed to be doing. Then, as the chapters progress, the explicit becomes the implicit, and then eventually becomes only the merest hint of a suggestion – or is even completely absent. You will need to use your experience from the earlier chapters to work out what is expected of you.

Of course, your existing experience and knowledge will inform your own perception of puzzle difficulty, so you will no doubt find some harder puzzles earlier on, and some surprisingly easy puzzles at the later stages of the book.

2. Making Progress

Every puzzle that doesn't already include explicit instructions will always include one really quite significant hint: its title. They may seem strange from time to time, but they are intended to help. Each title gives you a clue as to what is going on in that puzzle, or at the very least should let you know you're on the right path once you get going on the puzzle. So if the title doesn't make sense, stop and think about it – or, conversely, if you don't want a hint then *don't* think about it!

But when you get stuck – and you almost certainly *will* get stuck – then there are several things you can try:

- You could try *explaining* the puzzle to someone else, even if that someone is in fact you in your bathroom mirror. The simple act of putting your thoughts into words forces you to think about things from a new angle, and can often help you make a breakthrough.

- Keep going, and try another puzzle. Inspiration may strike when you least expect it.

- Sleep on it. This might sound unhelpful, but astonishingly your unconscious brain really does carry on thinking about puzzles and problems while you sleep, and you might 'magically' find the solution popping into your head on the very next day.

- Sneak a look at the solution. Or better still, get someone else to do so and then have them give you a hint rather than simply tell you the solution. You could also ask them specific questions, such as 'Does this involve anagrams?', 'Do I need to do something first before I connect the entries?', or 'Is it lunchtime yet?'. Stick closer to the first two examples if you are trying to make progress.

- Look for parts of the puzzle written in CAPITAL LETTERS. Yes, LIKE THIS. There's a reason I've done that, which is to indicate that the individual LETTERS are important. A common example of this is if the letters are to be anagrammed. Conversely, if the puzzle is formatted with regular use of upper and lower case, it consists of clues to words rather than literal letters to be manipulated in some way. There is the very occasional exception to this 'rule', however, where I felt you didn't need a hint.

- Most of the puzzles are fairly self-contained, but sometimes you will need external, real-world knowledge. Generally this is indicated in the question, although occasionally you have to deduce this – this is typically where a code is involved, and you must then research this code (online, or in a library, or even a book of your own possession) to deduce exactly how the puzzle is to be decoded. If there is some strange phrasing in a question, and there appears to be nowhere to make progress, then try googling the unusual terms.

- As the previous hint implied, it's not just the puzzle names that have hints in. The text does too, although not always. If something is oddly or unusually phrased, there's a reason for it. Or perhaps I just didn't get round to proofreading it. Probably the former, though.

- Ask your family, colleagues or indeed neighbours for help, or at least to read the puzzle for you and see if there's something you missed. It will, of course, help if you get stuck early on so they get a chance to learn how the puzzles work. Good luck asking them for help for the first time on the final puzzle!

• Finally, if you are still stuck, you could try getting some exercise. This will get your blood flowing, and speed up the flow of oxgyen to your brain so you can think faster. Plus, it feels great!

3. Specific Tips

Sometimes the general hints in the previous section will be simply *too* general. In such cases, try these things:

• Are anagrams involved?

• Are the starts or ends of words to be deleted? Or even the middle?

• If something isn't being deleted, is something being inserted?

• Are words or answers to clues related in terms of the letters in them? How do their word lengths relate? Are there common parts, or common sounds, or anything else you can see that is consistent across entries?

• Find a summary of common codes and signalling methods, and glance through to familiarize yourself with some standard terms.

• You will never unexpectedly require any obscure knowledge, since on the rare occasions where you do then you should *know* you need it – and in such a situation the puzzle is designed around the assumption that you *will* look up information. You aren't expected to know, for example, the names of every capital city, the title of every movie ever made, or the dots and dashes of every Morse code letter.

- Look for common sequences of letters within words, and also at the start or end of a word.

- If a puzzle involves a set of clues, then almost every puzzle has some deliberately easier and some deliberately trickier clues. The intention is that you work out how the puzzle is progressing from the easier clues, then use these to help you solve the trickier clues – similar to how a crossword clue gets easier to solve as you obtain crossing letters from other clues. So jump around a set of clues, and don't expect to necessarily be able to solve them in the order given.

4. Get Cracking

There's no time like the present! The first puzzle is on the very next page.

Good luck!

Dr Gareth Moore

Email: gareth@drgarethmoore.com
Twitter: @DrGarethMoore

Chapter 1:
Amusements

1. Linked Anagrams

Each of the following anagrams has something in common. Unscramble the anagrams, then find the theme that connects them all. There may be more than one possible anagram of some of the words, but only one of these will fit with the common theme.

- BROAD
- CAFE
- DEN
- DIMN
- DRAC
- FIAR
- GIB
- HEYROT
- LNAP
- YOB

2. Twenty or Less

Find sixteen whole numbers, none of them greater in value than twenty, in this word search grid. But beware – there is a twist. In this puzzle, there are no bounds on the grid, which wraps around in all directions as if it repeated forever at every border. One word is already solved, to help you get started.

3. Newly Named Novels

The following well-known novels have each been renamed in order to make their titles more alliterative.

What was the original name of each book? For example, *Boastfulness and Bigotry* could be the new name of *Pride and Prejudice*, were that title not alliterative already!

- Away with the Air
- The Berries of Bitterness
- Combat and Calm
- Courageous Contemporary Cosmos
- Creature Croft
- The Crimson Character
- Delinquency and Discipline
- The Fielder in the Field
- A Goodbye to Guns
- Huge Hopes
- Milky Molars

4. Speaking in Circles

You could be saved by the bell, if the bell did this.
And give me one for a chat, or for marital bliss.

What am I?

5. Square Loop

Draw horizontal and vertical lines to form a single loop that visits every white square in this grid exactly once each. The loop cannot touch or cross over itself at any point.

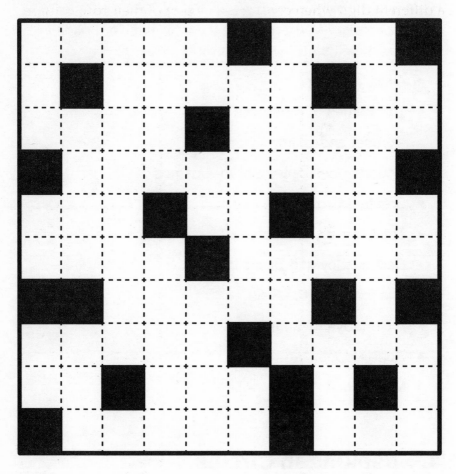

6. Black-out Sudoku

Place a digit from 1 to 9 into each white square so that every row, column and bold-lined 3×3 box contains eight different digits. The shaded squares remain blank, and may represent a different digit when considered as part of their row, column and box.

4		5			1		2	7
	6	3					4	
		7	9				6	
		6		7		8		3
			3		8			
8		9		4		7		
	8				3	4		
	2					5	3	
5	3		2			9		1

7. Movie Match-Up

Can you match up the two halves of these movie titles, each of which have an 'and' in between them?

An Officer		A Funeral
Antony		A Gentleman
Beauty		Automobiles
Bonnie		Cleopatra
Butch Cassidy		Clyde
Dazed		Confused
Dumb		Dolls
Four Weddings		Dumber
Guys	*and*	Guildenstern are Dead
Hannah		Her Sisters
Harold		I
Monty Python		Louise
Planes, Trains		Maude
Rosencrantz		Sensibility
Sense		The Beast
Sex, Lies		The Butterfly
The Diving Bell		The Holy Grail
The Good, the Bad		The Sundance Kid
Thelma		The Ugly
Withnail		Videotape

8. Presidential Mix-Up

The following are anagrams of the surnames of US presidents, with an extra letter added to each. Can you unscramble the anagrams and then anagram the extra letters to find an eleventh president?

- WINLOSE = _____ + __

- MADASH = _____ + __

- SCANJOKE = _____ + __

- CLEANLIVED = _____ + __

- HYENAS = _____ + __

- GLADFIRES = _____ + __

- FLOORMILE = _____ + __

- DOCILEEGO = _____ + __

- HOTWARNINGS = _____ + __

- VOTESLOWER = _____ + __

9. What Can You Do?

What can be done to all of the following?

- fall
- habit
- leg
- promise
- record
- rule

10. Daisy Chain

Can you complete the chain from DAISY to DAISY by rearranging the letters and changing one letter at each stage?

DAISY

_____	light yellowish-brown
_____	be on one's feet
_____	desires
_____	dried stalks of grain
_____	snares
_____	small pointed missiles
_____	piece of broken glass
_____	out of the sun

DAISY

11. What the Dickens?

Identify these Charles Dickens characters, each of which has had the letters of BLEAK HOUSE removed from their names.

- IVR TWIT

- DVID CPPRFID

- NZR CRG

- MI VIM

- NIC NICY

- MRTIN CZZWIT

- MGWITC

- FGIN

- RNY RDG

- YDNY CRTN

12. Back for Seconds

You buy a cake and cut it up into slices. You then eat half of the slices plus one. A little later, you return and eat half of the remaining slices plus one. Then, in a short while, you go back and eat half of the remaining slices plus one. You then return for a final time and eat half of the remaining slices plus one, after which point the cake is finished.

How many slices were there to start with?

13. Literary Logic

Three books have been returned to the library desk: *Across the Lake, One Hundred Degrees*, and *One Long Night*. One is a detective novel, one is a romance, and the third is science fiction. The three authors are Carter, Davies and Walker. The following are also true:

- Carter's book has a shorter title than the detective story.

- *One Long Night*'s author is earlier in the alphabet than the science fiction writer.

- The detective story has neither a 'D' in its title nor the name of its author.

Based on this information, can you deduce the author and genre of each book?

14. Dangerous Music

Can you fill in the links and identify the clued singer?

- MOTHER _____ QUAKE

- SWAN _____ SHEET

- BIG _____ AFFLECK

- DEAD _____ GENERATION

- LEG _____ GIRL

- GONE _____ APPLE

- JET _____ SHEEP

- EITHER _____ ELSE

- EGG _____ NOISE

15. Mixed Pictures

Each of these is an anagram of a one-word Academy Award for Best Picture winner, with two extra letters and a space. Can you unscramble the anagrams, and then unscramble the extra letters to find a sixth Best Picture winner?

- A CHORUS = _____ + __,__

- ACTING FIT = _____ + __,__

- HAND RING = _____ + __,__

- LATE ADORING = _____ + __,__

- SUAVE MAID = _____ + __,__

16. Dotty Loop

Draw horizontal and vertical lines to form a single loop that visits every dot exactly once each. The loop cannot touch or cross over itself at any point.

Some parts of the loop are already given.

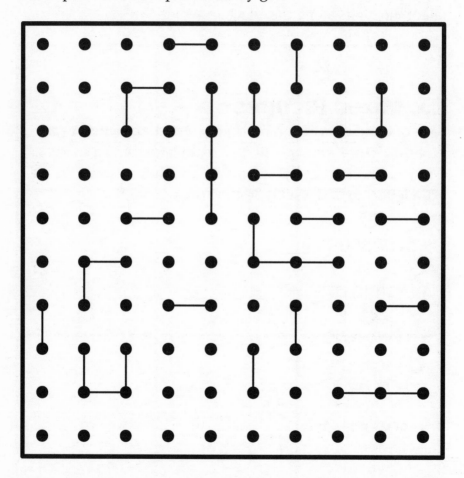

17. Arrow Sudoku

Place a digit from 1 to 9 into each white square so that every row, column and bold-lined 3×3 box contains nine different digits.

Any digit placed inside a circle must be equal to the sum of all of the digits along the attached arrow.

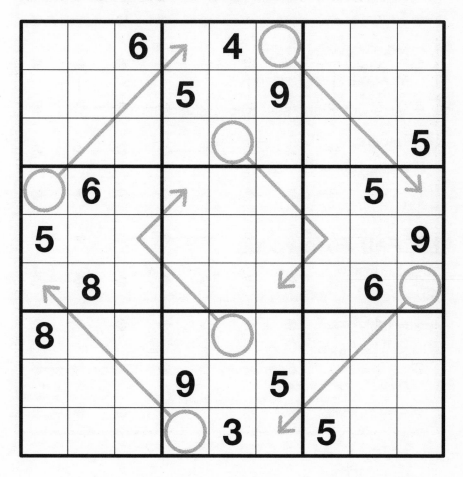

18. Pyramidal

The answer to each of the following clues contains the same letters as the previous word, plus one extra, although the order may be different. What are each of the words?

- Part of a play

- Informal conversation

- Educate

- Morally pure

- Most affectedly teasing

- More watertight, as a ship (archaically)

- Traders

- Writing skins

19. Fab Forewords

Can you unscramble the following words and then pair them up?

- ANELORE

- BERPACAKP

- BIRGY

- BREAMUINS

- DUEJ

- GEETROTH

- KACB

- LOWLEY
- MEOC
- NEAL
- NEPNY
- TEG
- TRIWER
- YEH

20. Easy as a Sequence

What comes next in this mathematical sequence?

1   4   1   5   9   2   6   _____

21. A Leg to Stand On

You're throwing a birthday party for your pet dog. Not including you and your dog there are 30 guests, some of whom are people and some of whom are dogs. All of the people have two legs and all of the dogs have four legs. Between them, they have 86 legs.

How many of the guests are dogs?

22. Wordoku

Reveal the hidden word by solving this sudoku puzzle. Place the letters A, D, E, O, P, R, S, T and W once each into every row, column and bold-lined 3×3 box. The secret word will be revealed along the shaded diagonal.

						T		
W					T	E		
			R	E	A			D
D		W					T	
S			T		E			O
	R					S		W
A			D	O	S			
		T	E					P
		O						

23. Reckoning by the Rules

The words in the following table have been sorted according to two rules, Rule A and Rule B. By examining the words in the table, can you deduce what these rules are, and then assign each of the extra words to the correct column?

Rule A	Rule B	Rules A and B	Neither A nor B
ORCHID	GRACE	POPPY	JANE
VIOLET	SALLY	DAISY	PLUM
AZALEA	FLEUR	ERICA	PEAR
PINK	ALICE	TANSY	MIRANDA

Extra words:

- CLOVER
- ELLEN
- IRIS
- SHARON

24. Word Net

Can you find the word 'HIDDEN', hidden somewhere in this word net? The letters of the word must be directly linked, in order, by one of the lines within the web.

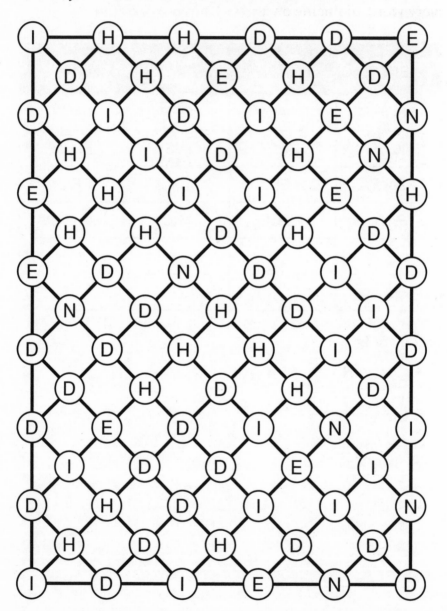

25. Ladies in Waiting

Each of the words in the left-hand column makes a new word when one of the names from the right-hand column is added to the end of them. Can you identify the new words, using every word and name once each?

• BAN	• AMY
• BIG	• ELLA
• COUNTER	• JO
• LIVE	• JOY
• OVER	• LILY
• SALMON	• MARY
• SUM	• SUE

26. Debugging Required

What do the following words all have in common?

- Beef
- Blouse
- Dismantle
- Godmother
- Smidgen
- Sniffly

27. Not a Band

The following names are the 'opposites' of real band names. Can you identify the real bands they are based on?

- Red Night
- Hotwork
- King
- The Black Spots
- The Herb Boys
- The White Locks
- The Windows
- The Stationary Sticks
- Videotail
- Yes Certainty

28. Ordered List

Rearrange these words in increasing order of value:

- Artwork
- Attention
- Homophone
- Puniness
- Weighted

29. Four-Letter Words

Can you make eight four-letter words, each beginning with
'S', by taking one letter from each column for each word, and
reading them from left to right?

The letters in each column have all been moved up or down
by a constant amount, wrapping from top to bottom and
vice-versa, so you won't need to keep reshuffling the letters in
each column to reveal all of the answers.

	I	A	D
	L	L	R
	N	G	F
S	Y	O	H
	O	U	G
	A	N	B
	C	D	C
	E	I	A

30. A Way with Words

What word can be added to the front of all of these words to
form a set of new words?

- GONE

- HOUSE

- MA

- WOOD

31. Proverb Ally

Some well-known proverbs have been rephrased. Can you work out what the original proverbs were?

- A resident of the largest country within the United Kingdom's place of residence is his fortified location

- If the footwear is of a suitable size, you should take make use of it

- The possession of currency is not all there is

- The man that is the final one to be audibly amused will also be the one who sustains this for the greatest amount of time

- Those who are not a fan of warm locations should leave the environs of cooking facilities

- Offences punishable by law are not remunerated

- Work-related events should take place prior to more relaxing activities

32. Time for Tea

Can you find all of these teas in the grid? They are all written in the shape of a 'T', although the 'T' may be at any rotation (except diagonally). One is already found, as an example.

```
H  N  V  E  I  A  D  I  M  B  U  U  Y  G  B
P  M  D  A  R  J  E  E  L  E  M  W  E  E  O
A  O  I  G  L  I  N  A  A  R  E  N  R  I  G
A  H  N  N  M  N  E  L  O  G  G  L  R  A  E
D  S  L  A  A  G  E  A  R  U  S  S  I  A  N
R  I  E  S  S  A  S  A  M  Y  E  C  K  E  E
M  L  B  R  E  A  K  F  A  S  T  A  G  M  N
N  G  U  N  A  H  L  E  E  A  R  R  L  U  R
U  N  A  N  A  T  O  O  N  G  I  A  O  N  O
Y  E  I  O  A  R  O  K  O  E  R  V  S  O  O
C  O  O  W  L  I  N  E  K  A  A  A  F  C  I
T  N  M  A  P  E  G  N  A  R  O  N  Y  V  B
E  O  A  M  I  L  E  J  I  Y  A  I  E  A  A
E  L  H  E  N  I  M  A  H  C  W  R  R  L  C
Y  E  C  N  Y  E  I  S  A  H  G  Y  D  A  L
```

- ASSAM
- CEYLON
- CHAI
- CHAMOMILE
- DARJEELING
- DIMBULA
- EARL GREY
- ENGLISH BREAKFAST
- GREEN
- JASMINE

- KEEMUN
- KENILWORTH
- LADY GREY
- MASALA
- NILGIRI
- OOLONG
- ORANGE PEKOE
- ROOIBOS
- RUSSIAN CARAVAN
- YUNNAN

33. First and Last

The same letter has been deleted from both the start and end of each of these words. Can you restore all of the original words?

- __RUI__
- __AXI__
- __DG__
- __EWTO__
- __EVE__
- __OOC__
- __EDAU__
- __GEND__
- __ATYR__
- __IOS__

34. Another Way with Words

What word can be added to the front of all of these words to form a set of new words?

- BREAK
- DREAM
- LIGHT
- TIME

35. Number Link

Draw a set of paths to link each pair of identical numbers. Paths can run horizontally or vertically between squares, but only one path can enter any square. Paths cannot touch or cross. A small solved example is shown.

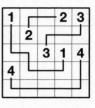

							1	2	3
		3							
							2	4	5
					1				
6		6							
									7
	8					9			
4		10				7		9	
8				5		10			

36. Quad Pencil-mark Sudoku

Place 1 to 9 once each in every row, column and bold-lined 3×3 box.

Some sets of four squares have four small digits written on the intersection between them. These four digits are to be assigned to those four squares, in some unknown order.

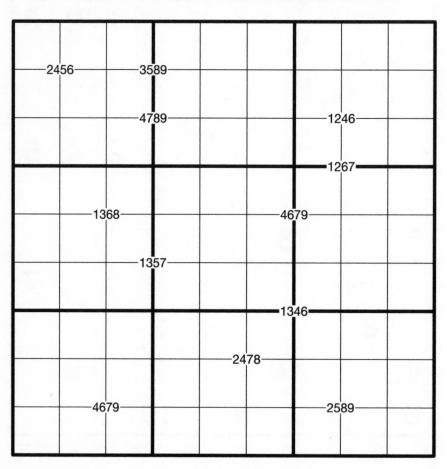

37. Sequel Sequence

What set of letters should come last, to complete this sequence?

- P S
- C O S
- P O A
- G O F
- O O T P
- H P
- _____

38. Worldly Letters

What should come next in the following real-world sequence?

- N
- U
- S
- J
- M
- E
- ___

39. Spiral Crossword

Fill this spiral crossword by solving each of the inward and the outward clues. Write one letter per box, starting from the numbered square.

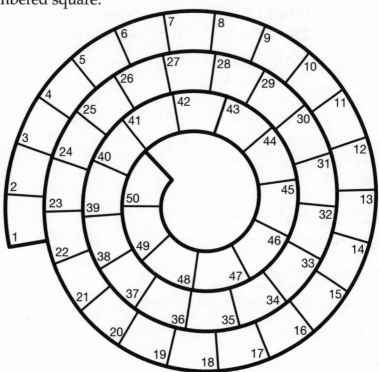

Inward

1-6	Relating to the mail
7-11	Knock over
12-19	Creating some early text
20-22	Sharp bite
23-28	Confuse
29-31	Maybes
32-34	Go bad
35-37	Short time (abbr)
38-42	Absolute low
43-47	Sunset to sunrise
48-50	Greek letter 'X's

Outward   50-46 One after fifth
45-43 Clear alcoholic spirit
42-40 Free
39-31 Forefathers
30-26 Land for growing crops
25-19 Depositing waste without permission
18-16 Bad hair discovery
15-13 Distant
12-8   Slaver
7-4   Level; smooth
3-1   Steep in liquid

40. Parts of a Whole

What connects the following clues?

- Item of clothing

- Higher place of education

- Computer

- Very brief unit of time

- Decorative light fitting

- Wine flavoured with aromatic herbs

- Having a golden yellow colour

41. Caesar Salad

Shift these letters by a constant amount to reveal some pertinent words:

- OHWWXFH

- FURXWRQV

- FKHHVH

- ZRUFHVWHUVKLUH VDXFH

42. Dice Decision

You have the following shape net:

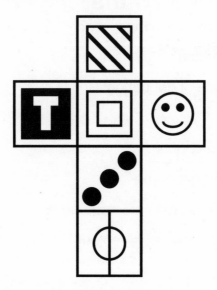

If you were to cut this out and fold it up to make a cube, which of the following would result?

43. Slightly Altered

Each of the following words has been altered according to the same rule. Work out the rule and find the word that connects them all.

- STICK
- DIWN
- UER
- CURA
- FEVA
- IOT

44. Relationship Study

This written extract describes an on-again off-again relationship. How does it end up? On, or off?

I felt abandoned. Officially she was away for work, but that was merely an illusion. When I rang her office they had not a notion where she was. She was a serial offender, of course, for she had done all this before.

She brought toffees with her when she returned. That was a Monday. I was angry, scoffing at her dishonest offering.

'You just keep going on at me!' she complained.

I stormed out of the room. When I had cooled off with a consoling coffee, I resolved myself and spoke to her.

'Honestly,' I said, 'this could be the last nail in the coffin of our relationship'.

45. Multi-gram

Can you find five anagrams of the following letters?

E I L N S T

46. Shady Challenge

An entry is missing from this sequence. Can you suggest a suitable extra phrase, and where it should be inserted?

- Hundred dollar bill
- Within radio range
- When I hurt myself I yell, owing to the pain
- Forbidding re-entry
- Rhythm and blues
- Against the wind I go

47. It's All Greek to Me

Reorder the letters in these words in order to discover a common property that unites them all:

- Poisoned
- Shade
- Atrophied
- Holies
- Ears
- Syphon
- Heater
- Sore

48. Initial Movies List

Some major film titles are listed below, but only their initials are given. Can you identify each of the movies?

- BCATSK

- ESOTSM

- LSATSB

- OFOTCN

- OUATITW

- ROTLA

- TGTBATU

- TLOTRTTT

49. Country Codes

Can you identify each of the following countries?

- χ LE

- M
  ACO

- STINE $\rightarrow$ STINE $\leftarrow$

- N / WAY

- SIN . . . . ORE

- UG+A

- K I N G D O M → KINGDOM ←

- TIMOR   → TIMOR ←

-

50. Disemvowelled

All of the vowels have been deleted from the following Hollywood actors, and the spacing of their names has been changed. Can you identify all of the original names?

- B RDP TT

- GNK L LY

- J MSD N

- J HNN YD PP

- CL NF RT H

- TM HN KS

- MRL NBR ND

- LPCN

- GR GCLN Y

51. Outside Sudoku

Place 1 to 9 once each into every row, column and bold-lined 3×3 box within this puzzle grid.

Numbers outside the grid must be placed into one of the nearest three squares in the same row or column. If there is more than one number, the order they are inserted into the grid might not match the order they are given in.

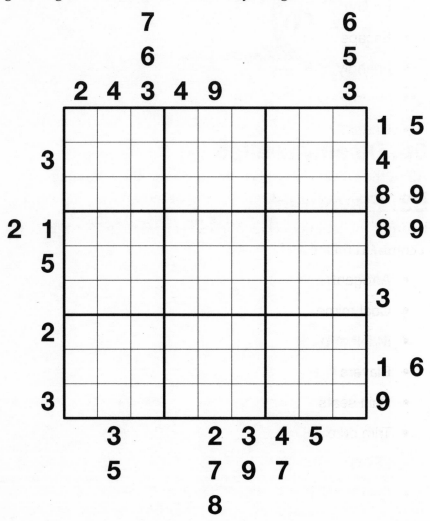

52. Hot Stuff

Can you divide the following words into two groups of four, according to a common theme?

- Alarm
- Breathe
- Drill
- Engine
- Escape
- Friendly
- Open
- Under

53. Flavoursome

Reorder the letters in each of these entries in order to discover a common theme.

- Arrogant
- Coal mime
- Major arm
- Players
- Rain seats
- Trim cure

54. Parking Fine?

In which of these words is there room for me to park?

- PRECARIOUS

- INNATE

- MASCARPONE

- SCARLET

- VICAR

- UNCARING

- SCARY

- MACARONI

55. Reading Query

What interesting property connects all of the following words?

- DECAY

- CUTIE

- OBEDIENCY

- ANEMONE

- SEEDY

- ESCAPEE

- EXCESS

56. Calcudoku

Place 1 to 8 once each into every row and column.

Each bold-lined region must result in the value given at its top-left when the operation given in the same location is applied between all of the numbers in that region.

For subtraction and division, start with the largest number in the region and subtract or divide by the remaining numbers in the region.

1−	9+			20×		15+	
	40×	64×		270×	42×		5−
360×							
		112×			3−		180×
	35×		16×				
56×		21+			2÷	10×	
	21×						4−
4÷		30×		18+			

57. First Puzzle

What is the first connection you can find between the solutions to all of the following clues?

- Street intersection
- Common type of puzzle
- Converging bullets from multiple locations
- Medieval weapon
- Product with success in multiple genres

58. Final Puzzle

What property unites all of the following words?

- HEAVEN
- QUARTZ
- WEARY
- DIVERSE
- CAMEL
- BADGER
- DAISY

Chapter 2
Diversions

1. Mixed Doubles

Can you unscramble each of these anagrams, then find a way to pair them so that they all adhere to a common theme?

- ABELT

- BXO

- DAHN

- DEEPS

- GIHH

- GLON

- ORW

- RIFUGE

- TEKABS

- WALN

2. Five by Five

Arrange the following items into five groups of five. Some items may fit into more than one category, but there is only one arrangement in which each category contains exactly five items and all items are assigned. It is up to you to discover what those categories are.

- LINCOLN
- ATHENS
- MUNICH
- CHEETAH
- TRUMP
- TOYOTA
- MINI
- BUSH
- GARFIELD
- MOSCOW
- HOOVER
- RIGA
- LEOPARD
- BMW
- LION
- MINORITY REPORT
- HOOK
- TIGER
- PARIS
- JAGUAR
- BRIDGE OF SPIES
- PUMA
- HONDA
- FORD
- ROME

3. Reckoning by the Rules

The words in the following table have been sorted according to two rules, Rule A and Rule B. By examining the words in the table, can you deduce what these rules are, and then assign each of the extra words to the correct column?

Rule A	Rule B	Rules A and B	Neither A nor B
RED	SILVER	ORANGE	PINK
GREEN	PURPLE	YELLOW	GOLD
BLUE	MAROON	VIOLET	AMBER
		INDIGO	NAVY

Extra words:

- BLACK
- COPPER
- WHITE
- SALMON

4. A Sweeping Statement

Dig a deep hole and you might find some ores...
...but keep your hands off – this isn't yours!

What is it?

5. Riddle

What word becomes longer when a letter is removed?

6. Snake

Can you find the snake in the following grid? The head and tail of the snake are given, but it is up to you to find the rest of it. Some rows and columns are numbered, and these indicate how many squares in that row or column are visited by the snake. An example solved puzzle is shown to the right.

A snake is a continuous path of squares that runs from the head to the tail, and which does not touch another part of the snake at any point, including diagonally. ('Another part' means a part of the snake more than two squares away along the length of the snake).

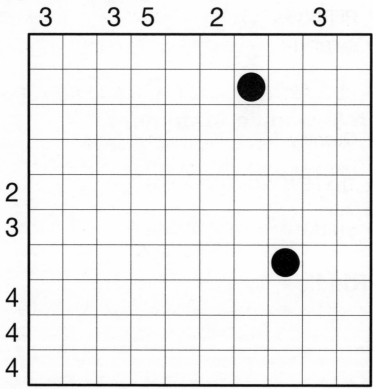

7. A Leading Question

Can you work out which letter should come next in the following written sequence?

C Y W O W L S C N I T F W _____

8. What's in a Name?

Identify each of the four following Shakespeare plays. Each is described using either visual clues or word play.

- ARTHUR   GAWAIN   GERAINT   LANCELOT

  PERCIVAL   BORS   KAY   LAMORAK

  GARETH   GAHERIS   GALAHAD   <u>BEDIVERE</u>

- ADO ADO ADO ADO 0 ADO ADO ADO ADO

- Quantify: 80cm, 6oz, 45ml, 100kg ¢

- The FEW WORD VISIONS

- SNIUGHMTSMDREEAMR

9. Jigsaw Box

Place 1 to 9 once each in every row, column, bold-lined jigsaw shape *and* 3×3 white or grey box region.

7							6	8
5								
			8	4	9			
			3		5			
			6	2	7			
								4
8	1							9

10. Linked Anagrams Too

Each of the following anagrams has something in common. Unscramble the anagrams, then find the theme that connects them. There may be multiple valid anagrams of some of the words, but only one of these will fit to the common theme.

- AREFUTE

- HIDS

- HINDLOG

- KACB

- KARM

- NUDER

- PEED

- THO

- VEELL

- WOND

11. Number Targets

Each of the target numbers can be made by summing two or more of the following numbers, without repeating a number more than once. How do you reach each target?

23   7   19   9   20   21   15

Targets:

- 40

- 53

- 61

- 76

- 90

12. Pyramidal Too

The answer to each of the following clues contains the same letters as the previous word, plus one extra, albeit possibly in a jumbled order. What are each of the words?

- Rodent
- Small arrow
- Walk
- Angry outburst
- Standing across
- Most robust
- Having lost its lustre
- Cause to lose determination
- Myopic

13. What Ls?

Can you find all of the listed words in the grid? They are all written in the shape of an 'L', although the 'L' may read from the head to tail, or the tail to the head. They are not rotated.

```
B Y P R L Y L R L A L L B L E
L L O E L L E V E L R L S L L
U L L F Y L L E B L I E Y I D
E I A L L A A Y R E G L L A B
B B E A O C I K L N A L L I V
E L L I H I V U L L A Y O J I
O V D U L B A L L Y S Y L O P
L O I L Y B L L E G E D L Y I
Y L A E L L A C I S S A L C V
L L L E C T A L F E L L S A A
L E E B L L L E L Y B A L L L
A Y F E L L L K I L L L E B L
I B E L I L S I H L A I L I F
C A L L H E L O M A G E L L I
A L G F L O W E R L O O D Y L
```

- ALLEGEDLY
- ALLELUIA
- ALLUVIAL
- BALLGIRL
- BELLFLOWER
- BELL-LIKE
- BELLYFLOP
- BLUEBELL
- CLASSICALLY
- DIALECTAL
- DOOLALLY
- FILIALLY
- FLYBALL
- GLACIALLY
- HILLBILLY
- ILLEGALLY
- JOLLY
- LEVELLER
- MOLEHILL
- POLYSYLLABICALLY
- VILLANELLA
- VOLLEYBALL

14. Movie Match-Up 2

Can you match up the two halves of each of these movie titles, all of which require an 'in' between them?

Alice		10 Days
A Place		60 Seconds
Around the World		80 Days
Barefoot		Beverly Hills
Big Trouble		Little China
Death		Love
Down and Out		Paris
Ghost		Pink
Gone		Seattle
Gorillas		The Iron Mask
How to Lose a Guy	*in*	The Mist
Last Tango		The Park
Lost		The Rain
Once Upon a Time		The Shadows
Pretty		The Shell
Shakespeare		The Sun
Singin'		The West
Sleepless		Translation
The Man		Venice
What We Do		Wonderland

15. Word Tree

Can you complete this word tree by finding the common word between each pair of linked boxes? Once you have found both of the linked words in the central column, add an extra word between these two words to reveal a well-known movie reading down the centre column.

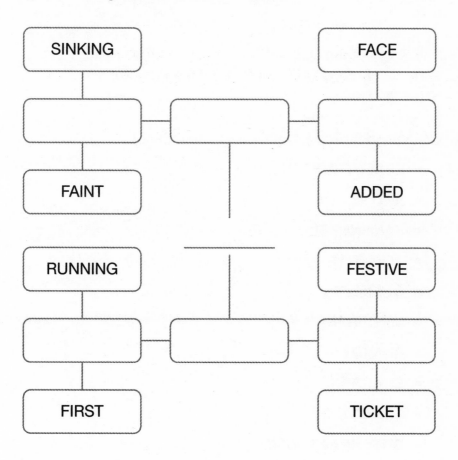

SINKING

FACE

FAINT

ADDED

RUNNING

FESTIVE

FIRST

TICKET

16. Game of Two Halves

The following are famous duos whose names have been woven together by taking the first letter of the first member of the duo, the second letter of the second, the third letter of the first, the fourth letter of the second, and so on, with any spare letters from the longer name left in their original order at the end.

The letters of the first name are given in **bold**. So, for example, 'Scooby Doo and Shaggy' would become **SHOGBYDOO**.

Can you identify each of the following duos?

- **PEALUTBUTTER**
- **ALTONATRA**
- **SAMFNNKEL**
- **AOBTTLLO**
- **GULLEVTN**
- **MHCERENI**
- **RUMIOT**
- **SUACSKY**
- **LCNAOTNEY**
- **BHTSHNAASCDKID**
- **DRJYKELL**
- **WRLMATE**

17. Lost in Austen

Identify these Jane Austen characters, each of which has had the letters of PRIDE AND PREJUDICE removed from their names.

- LZBTH BT
- OH WLLOGHBY
- MM WOOHOS
- FTZWLLM Y
- GOG KGHTLY
- TH BOGH
- HLS BGLY
- LO SHWOO
- GOG WKHM
- W FS

18. Pale Colours

All of the vowels have been stolen from the following shades of pink. Can you restore the original colours?

- RS
- CRL
- FCHS
- CRNTN
- PCH

19. Skyscraper

Place a number from 1 to 6 into each row and column within the grid of this skyscraper puzzle. These numbers represent skyscrapers of between 1 and 6 floors respectively.

<table>
<tr><td></td><td>3</td><td></td><td>2</td><td>2</td><td>2</td><td></td><td></td></tr>
<tr><td>4</td><td>2</td><td>1</td><td>4</td><td>3</td><td>5</td><td>6</td><td></td></tr>
<tr><td></td><td>3</td><td>5</td><td>1</td><td>6</td><td>4</td><td>2</td><td>3</td></tr>
<tr><td>3</td><td>1</td><td>3</td><td>6</td><td>5</td><td>2</td><td>4</td><td>3</td></tr>
<tr><td></td><td>6</td><td>4</td><td>5</td><td>2</td><td>3</td><td>1</td><td>4</td></tr>
<tr><td></td><td>5</td><td>6</td><td>2</td><td>4</td><td>1</td><td>3</td><td>3</td></tr>
<tr><td>2</td><td>4</td><td>2</td><td>3</td><td>1</td><td>6</td><td>5</td><td></td></tr>
<tr><td></td><td>3</td><td></td><td>3</td><td></td><td></td><td></td><td></td></tr>
</table>

Clue numbers at one end of a row or column give the the number of visible skyscrapers that can be seen from that point.

A skyscraper is visible if no taller skyscraper precedes it in the same row or column, reading from the direction of the clue. In the example, the '3' at the top corresponds to the 2, 3 and 6 in the column below, with the 1, 5 and 4 being hidden.

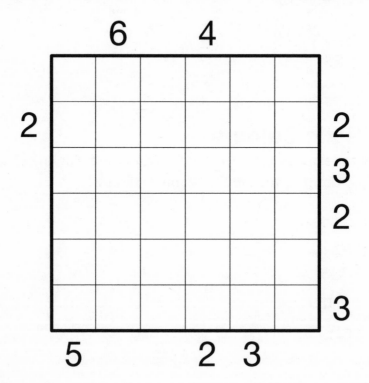

20. Platinum Albums

Can you work out the exact way in which each of these song titles has been changed? What was the original title of each song?

- ANTIMONYY DANCER, by Elton John
- COBALTIC, by Alanis Morissette
- COPPERS AND DIMES, by Dolly Parton
- FOLLOW MY BISMUTH, by Justin Timberlake
- MERCURY DIGGER, by Kanye West
- SODIUM, by John Mayer
- VANADIUM, by David Guetta

21. Secret Ingredients

What are the secret ingredients that these words conceal?

- Non-ionic
- Unicorn
- Psalter
- Automaton
- Caribbean
- Price

22. Killer Confusion Sudoku

Place 1 to 9 once each into every row, column and bold-lined 3×3 box of this puzzle. In addition, the numbers placed into each dashed-line cage must result in the given value when one of the four mathematical operations, +, −, × or ÷, is applied between all of the numbers in that region.

For subtraction and division, start with the largest number in the dashed-line cage and then subtract or divide by each of the remaining numbers.

23. Forbidden Planets

Can you find the six planets hidden in these sentences?

- Why does my oven usually overcook everything?

- The salsa turned from red to green.

- The politician was inept, unelectable, and afraid of any nuclear threat.

- Some Spanish grammar sounds different in the Honduran usage.

24. Nice and Easy

Identify the words being defined here, and deduce their common theme.

- All the same (12)

- Came down (9)

- Fizzy (12)

- In another place (9)

- Large burial ground (8)

- Respected and admired (8)

- Sports official (7)

- Urgent need for assistance (9)

25. Fruit Bowl

Place the list of fruit into the table, so that each fruit reads left to right in a continuous row of boxes, one letter per box. Everywhere a letter is shared between adjacent rows, the box is expanded to cover all of these rows. **One fruit is placed twice.**

The fruits to be placed are:

- APPLE
- APRICOT
- AVOCADO
- BLACKBERRY
- CHERRY
- CURRANT
- FIG
- GUAVA
- KIWI
- LEMON
- LIME
- LOGANBERRY
- LOQUAT
- MANGO
- MELON
- NECTARINE
- OLIVE
- PAPAYA
- PAWPAW
- PEACH
- PEAR
- PINEAPPLE
- PLUM
- POMEGRANATE
- TOMATO

26. Up-front Query

What connects the following words?

- COVERAGE
- GRUMBLE
- LAWFUL
- ORANGE
- WOMEN

27. Word Tour

Can you complete this international word ladder, by changing one letter at each stage? Do not otherwise rearrange the letters.

_____	**Tehran's country**
_____	edible seed coat
_____	legume
_____	long piece of timber
_____	group working together
_____	period of tenure
_____	give hair a wave
_____	**Lima's country**
_____	stick up jauntily
_____	meat from a pig
_____	opening in the skin
_____	untainted
_____	heal
_____	power of three
_____	**Havana's country**

28. Cinema Conundrum

There's a special offer on movie tickets at the cinema, so you're going to see three movies in one day: *On The Run*, *Low Profile* and *Undercover*.

One movie is 90 minutes long, one is 120 minutes long, and one is 150 minutes long. Moreover, one is showing at 12pm, one at 3pm, and one at 6pm.

You also know the following facts:

- *Undercover* is showing before the 120 minute movie.
- The movie at 12pm is longer than *On The Run*.
- The 150 minute movie has multiple words in its title.

Deduce from this information both the duration of each movie and the time at which it is showing.

29. What Can You Do Too?

What can be done to all of the following?

- car
- mile
- race
- risk
- bath
- temperature

30. The Second First and Last

The same letter has been deleted from both the start and end of each of these words. Can you restore all of the original words?

- __NAC__
- __IL__
- __EARL__
- __ADA__
- __INNO__
- __OLY__
- __EO__
- __UZ__
- __AG__
- __ARVA__
- __AI__

31. Fly Away

What do the following words have in common?

- Alternate
- Antithesis
- Dovetail
- Knowledge
- Letterhead

- Probing
- Swanky
- Swiftly

32. Get the Picture

Pair up the following words according to a common theme. One word will be used in two pairs.

- Ago
- Brave
- Chic
- Heart
- Light
- Moon
- On
- Pat
- Plato
- Spot
- Ton

33. Frame Sudoku

Place 1 to 9 once each into every row, column and bold-lined 3×3 box within this puzzle grid.

Numbers outside the grid reveal the total of the nearest three digits in the same row or column.

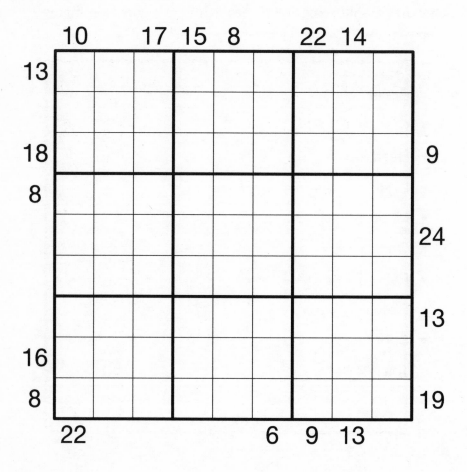

34. Touchy

Place one letter into each empty square so that every row and column contains all of the letters from A to H.

You must place letters so that identical letters do not touch diagonally. (They can't touch horizontally or vertically either, but this is already a requirement in order to place one of each letter into every row and column).

G	F						B
	B					G	A
			H				
			C	G	D		
		G	B	A			
				F			
D	C					E	
A						C	H

35. Men of Letters

The words in the left-hand column all make new words when a name from the right-hand column is added somewhere in the middle of them. Can you identify all of the new words?

- CAR
- CARD
- CARING
- CATS
- CUSS
- ENVIED
- PARENT
- REED
- RUFFS
- SEE

- ALAN
- DAVE
- IAN
- JACK
- LIAM
- MARK
- PETE
- RON
- SAM
- TOM

36. Rain Check

Sort these eight words into two groups, each of four words, according to a common theme.

- ALLEY
- BURGLAR
- DAYS
- DIRTY
- FAT

- FLAP

- HOT

- WHISTLE

37. Bookending

Each word in the first list can become a new word when a two-letter pair from the second list is added to the beginning and end of it. Can you match them all up?

Words	Two-letter pairs
ABLE	EN
ANTI	ER
AS	ES
AT	IC
CAP	LE
GIB	ME
I	ON
LIGHT	OR
ON	ST

38. Special Pairs

What is special about the following pairs of words?

- COURTEOUS and CURT

- FABRICATED and FACT

- COMMUNICATIVE and MUTE

39. Movie Match-Up

Can you match up the two halves of these movie titles, each
of which have a 'with' in between them?

A Room		Andre
Dances		A Vampire
Friends		A View
From Russia		Bashir
Fun		Benefits
Gone		Boys
Interview		Dick and Jane
My Dinner		Fire
One Night	*with*	Love
Riding in Cars		Morrie
Running		My Aunt
Sleeping		Scissors
The Girl		Steve Zissou
The Life Aquatic		The Dragon Tattoo
The Man		The Enemy
They're Playing		The Golden Gun
Travels		The King
Tuesdays		The Wind
Waltz		Wolves
You Can't Take It		You

40. More Newly Named Novels

The following well-known novels have each been renamed in order to make their titles more alliterative.

What was the original name of each book? For example, *Boastfulness and Bigotry* could be the new name of *Pride and Prejudice*, were that title not alliterative already!

- The Period of Purity

- The Resonance and the Rage

- The Servant's Story

- The Sizeable Snooze

- The Small Sovereign

- A Space with a Sight

41. May Contain Nuts

Each of these words contains an ingredient that some might need to avoid. Why?

- Diminutive

- Bootlegger

- Oafishness

- Blow-dryer

- Boatswain

42. Proverbial Problem

Some well-known proverbs have been rephrased. Can you work out what the original proverbs were?

- If you do something kind for another person then you will not fail to suffer the unfortunate consequences

- The compass point on the right, if north is at the top, is the same as itself, while the one that is diametrically opposed to that first point is itself the same as itself

- Requirements are the maternal parent of the creative process

- Be sure not to dispose of the infant along with the contents of a wash tub

- The passage of temporal reality is efficacious in its palliative effects

- The sample print for the dessert is located within the tasting

- Financial assets are the original source of all iniquity

43. Facing Off

The face is missing from one of these four cubes. Which of the faces shown beneath should replace the blank face, so that all four views could then be showing the same cube?

The possible faces are:

44. An Odd Scramble

One of these anagrammed entries is the odd one out. Which one?

- COOL CIDER

- NINE PUG

- CHECK-IN

- SOLAR TABS

- FINAL MOG

- SANE PATH

- COST TREACHERY

- GENIAL THING

45. Spiral Crossword

Fill this spiral crossword by solving each of the inward and the outward clues. Write one letter per box, starting from the numbered square.

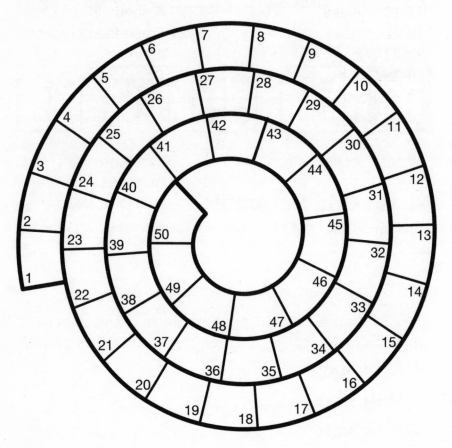

Inward

1-5	Tropical trees
6-9	Cathedral recess
10-13	Decomposes
14-18	Mistake
19-22	Edges
23-27	Sulky
28-30	Metal-bearing mineral
31-35	Polite
36-39	Boundary
40-45	Doorkeeper
46-50	Circular paths

Outward

50-46	Reel
45-41	Like a blast from the past
40-38	A short pin or bolt
37-34	Fresh-food products counter
33-27	Sovereign's stand-in
26-22	Condemns
21-16	Looking glass
15-9	Return to original condition
8-4	Sudden convulsion
3-1	Drink like a dog

46. Vowel Play

The vowels have been deleted from the following national airlines, and the spacing has been changed. Can you identify all of the flag carriers?

- RLN GS

- J PNR LN S

- LTL

- B RTS HRW YS

- QNTS

- LF THN S

- LL

47. Alternative Puzzle

What is odd about the following words?

- CALLIOPES

- PAINED

- SCHOOLED

- TRIENNIALLY

48. Hanjie Sudoku

What is the odd number out in this combination puzzle?

- Solve as a sudoku, ensuring each row and column of squares, plus each 3×3 bold-lined box of squares, contains 1 to 9 once each.

- The numbers outside the grid act firstly as extra sudoku clues that refer only to the 3×3 square they are next to. Each of these numbers must be placed into its matching row or column of the nearest 3×3 square, although not necessarily in the order given.

- Solve also as a hanjie puzzle, where the numbers around the outside are also secondly instructions on how to shade the grid. A single number means that there is a continuous block of that many shaded cells in that row or column. Two numbers means that there are two blocks of that many shaded cells in that row or column, separated by at least one unshaded square. These blocks are in the order that the clues appear.

- Lastly, find the odd number out in the unshaded region.

		9	8	7	1 6	2 5	3 4	4 3	5 2	6 1
	9		6	5	7	8				
	8	4								7
	7	2					9			
1	6		9			7			3	
2	5			8	9		1	7		
3	4		7			6			9	
4	3				2					5
5	2	8								9
6	1					4	8	2	7	

49. Clue Connects

What connects the solutions to the following clues?

- The most computer-obsessed

- One who lives in a place

- Added to the middle

- Fashionable people

50. Five by Five Two

Arrange the following items into five groups of five. Some items may fit into more than one category, but there is only one arrangement in which each category contains exactly five items and all items are assigned. It is up to you to discover what those categories are.

- SARAH
- VULCAN
- SWIFT
- GOLD
- SWALLOW
- NEPTUNE
- KIWI
- DIANA
- FLORA
- EARTH
- COPPER
- MARS
- MERCURY
- JANE
- CRANE
- PHOEBE
- VENUS
- SILVER
- SATURN
- CERES
- TIN
- ANDREA
- VIOLA
- FAUNA
- PENGUIN

51. Hide Away

Can you find all of these words in the grid? They are all found in straight lines, running in any direction.

Part of the grid is missing. It's up to you to restore it.

```
D A R K E N O L S E C R E T E
R L D I S G U I S E B E S O E
D S T O R E A T L U S T D S O
L A E C N O C L R C E T P I T
O R M R R E L Y F R L I O H H
H G P U R           L O G W S
H S K R U           O I U O S
T H R E V           S M B D E
I R S A E           T S A S R
W O T C E           T L H C P
C U L E R L D T C R K A E M P
L D K I E E U A U S D A A H U
O V B I E O E C R O B S T K S
A O L S L V T N W K K O W O U
K G O T O G R O U N D E W O B
```

- BURY
- CAMOUFLAGE
- CLOAK
- CLOUD
- CONCEAL
- COVER UP
- DARKEN
- DISGUISE
- ECLIPSE
- GO TO GROUND
- HIDE
- KEEP DARK
- KEEP SECRET
- LIE LOW
- LURK
- MASK
- OBSCURE
- OBSTRUCT
- OUT OF SIGHT
- SCREEN
- SECRETE
- SHADOW
- SHELTER
- SHROUD
- STORE
- STOW
- SUPPRESS
- TAKE COVER
- VEIL
- WITHHOLD

52. Must Dash

Read this extract and decode the urgent alert it is conveying.

Dotty dotingly told me an anecdote. It was about a dashing man in Bermuda shorts, who had plenty of cash, but his manner was a little slapdash. She said she did not care, but I think the lady doth protest too much – she must need an antidote for her strong feelings or else she may cross the dreaded dotted line!

53. Winter Clothing

Dress each of these sets of letters in order to make complete words and phrases:

- _ _ LD SWE _ _
- _ _ SBEGO _ _ _ _
- _ _ BI _
- _ _ _ _ E OF _
- _ ARLIC C _ _ _ _

54. Popular Initials

Which well-known pop songs do these initials stand for? Each is listed along with its performing band/artist.

- BOTW by SAG
- DQ by A
- EOTT by S

- IHITTG by MG
- IWALY by WH
- RATC by BHATC
- RITD by A
- YSV by CS

55. Multi-gram Again

Can you find five anagrams of the following letters?

A D E H R S T

56. Vowel Play

All of the vowels have been deleted from these street signs, and the spaces rearranged. Can you restore them?

- SP DLM T
- MR GLNS
- R DW RKS
- G VW Y
- D DN D
- SL WDW N
- ST PNC LN

57. Further Country Codes
Can you identify these countries?

- CO  ICA

- D A I

- R 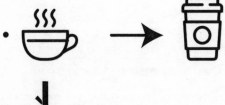 A

- S ♥ NIA

- S *ow!*

-  → ⬒

- Ⓠ*R*Y

58. Timely Sequence
What comes next in the following sequence of numbers?

- 0 3 0 1 0 1 0 0 1 0 1 ___

59. Sky Movies

What links the following films?

- Butch Cassidy and the Sundance Kid

- Gone with the Wind

- Hail, Caesar!

- Rain Man

- Snow White and the Seven Dwarves

60. Train Timetable

You wish to catch a train to Shelltown. There are three trains leaving for Shelltown in the next twenty minutes: one at 13:10, one at 13:15 and one at 13:30. One is leaving from Platform One, one from Platform Two and one from Platform Three. One will take 40 minutes, one will take 50 minutes, and one will take an hour to get there.

- The train from Platform 1 is quicker than the 13:15 train.

- The 50-minute train leaves later than the train from Platform 3.

- The 40-minute train has a lower platform number than the 13:10 train.

Based on this information, can you deduce which train will get you there the soonest?

61. Product Frame Sudoku

Place 1 to 6 once each into every row, column and bold-lined 3×2 box within this puzzle grid.

Numbers outside the grid reveal the product of the digits in the same row or column that are also within the nearest 3×2 box. In other words, numbers to the left or right of the grid give the product of the three nearest numbers in the same row, while numbers above or below the grid give the product of the two nearest numbers in the same column.

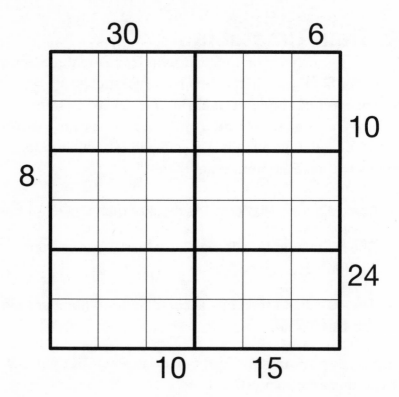

Chapter 3
Challenges

1. Capital Stock

What do the following capital cities have in common?

- Antananarivo
- Ashgabat
- Athens
- Bratislava
- Bucharest
- Khartoum
- Moscow
- Muscat
- Paramaribo
- Rabat

2. Word Tree Too

Can you complete this word tree by finding the common word between each pair of linked boxes? Once you have found both of the linked words in the central column, add an extra word between these two words to reveal a well-known movie reading down the centre column.

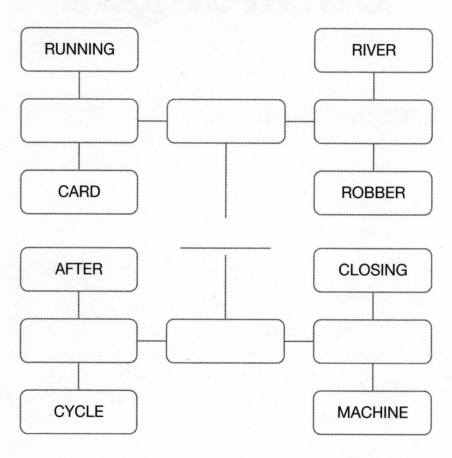

3. Reckoning by the Rules 3

The countries in the table below have been sorted according to two rules, Rule A and Rule B. By examining the countries in the table, can you first of all deduce what these rules are, and then assign each of the extra countries to its correct column?

Rule A	Rule B	Rules A and B	Neither A nor B
SEYCHELLES	CROATIA	GREECE	ECUADOR
CAMEROON	POLAND	ANDORRA	CUBA
PHILIPPINES	DENMARK	RUSSIA	AUSTRALIA
MARSHALL ISLANDS	GERMANY		INDIA
GUINEA-BISSAU			

Extra countries:

- MOROCCO
- FRANCE
- INDONESIA

4. A Pressing Matter

An attack that's at a cost, and an accusation.

If battery's the problem, do this for a duration. What is it?

5. The Late Shift

Julius has been working later and later recently. In fact, his shift has been an hour later every day for the past eight days. He's getting so tired that his thoughts are becoming incoherent. He's written down one letter each day.

He now has: IQPI YOTM

What is Julius really thinking about?

6. More Number Targets

Each of the target numbers can be made by summing two or more of the following numbers, without repeating a number more than once. How do you reach each target?

11   25   10   13   24   9   15

Targets:

- 28
- 40
- 55
- 67
- 75

7. Hidden Path

Can you find a hidden path in the following
grid? The start and end of the path are given,
but it is up to you to find the rest of it. Some
rows and columns are numbered, and these
indicate how many dots in that row or column

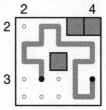

form part of the path. An example solved puzzle is shown to
the right.

The path runs only runs horizontally or vertically between
neighbouring dots, and does not cross over any of the shaded
blocks.

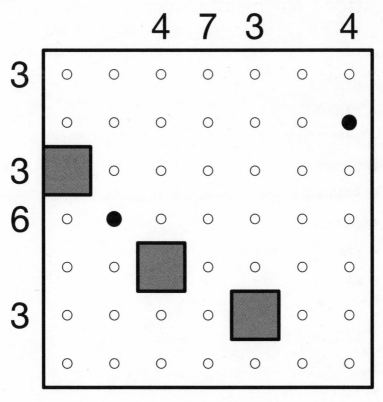

8. Body of Information

The words in this list all have some relation to a common theme. They form four groups of four, whereby each group relates to the common theme in a different way.

For example, if the common theme was fish, one category might be words that contain fish, e.g. UNFOR<u>TUNA</u>TE, and another might be first names of people whose surnames are fish, e.g. JACKSON (Pollock).

Can you divide these words into their four groups?

- FEAT
- GREEN
- HARE
- KEENS
- KNOWS
- POTATOES
- RAMS
- SAVING
- SEAR
- SHAKE
- SMUG
- SPARE
- SPLASHES
- TULIPS
- VERMOUTH
- WASTE

9. Spectator Sports

Identify each of the five following Olympic sports. Each is described using either visual clues or word play.

- NISNISNISNISNISNISNISNISNISNIS

-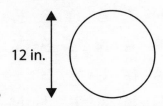

- TINNOM

- 12 in. ⃝

10. Late-breaking Puzzle

What is special about the following words?

- ATTENDANCE

- OFTENTIMES

- TOMORROW

- TOREADOR

11. Cross Words

Can you find all of these words in the grid? They are all found in crosses ('+' or 'x' shapes), where the middle of the cross is used twice by the word.

S	I	E	R	N	T	S	Y	I	A	D	H	A	O	H
M	A	A	S	T	U	H	A	N	O	B	L	R	L	R
C	P	R	H	S	R	R	M	T	I	N	E	O	O	R
R	G	O	N	S	R	A	I	B	E	L	H	B	W	W
U	C	A	Y	I	T	C	R	C	F	D	A	N	O	S
S	H	H	R	F	L	A	U	S	C	O	R	P	R	I
G	S	A	C	K	Y	A	A	I	A	N	H	L	Y	C
E	B	D	L	S	A	S	T	R	E	A	S	K	U	S
T	N	A	R	I	K	R	A	D	T	D	C	S	B	A
I	N	T	K	R	C	T	R	B	A	N	U	B	Y	E
P	I	C	U	A	U	S	M	A	M	C	A	S	E	S
E	C	O	J	O	L	N	Y	R	K	A	L	I	N	V
K	L	N	O	G	L	M	L	S	C	H	A	I	T	K
D	U	V	T	H	I	A	O	S	C	E	A	S	S	O
B	E	M	E	S	B	C	D	S	L	K	T	T	A	B

- ALKALI
- ANOINT
- ASSIST
- BALLAD

- BANTAM
- BELIEF
- BORROW
- BUNKUM

- BYE-BYE
- CAESAR
- CASUAL
- CITRIC
- CORDON
- COSMOS
- DENIED
- EVOLVE
- FLATLY
- HANGAR
- HOLLOW
- INDENT
- INVENT
- JACKAL
- OUTRUN
- PARIAH
- PICNIC
- PRIORY
- RHYTHM
- SCARCE
- SCORCH
- SKULKS
- SMARMY
- STRATA
- STUNTS
- THIGHS

12. New World

Recently, I travelled around the world. I saw an animal in the Philippines, visited a plaza in Bolivia, went to some saunas in the Bahamas, and squashed a louse in South Korea. Which part of a plant did I pluck in Iran?

13. Read Between the Lines

Fill in the blanks in the example from each of these seven
different categories, and then work out how to place them all
into order.

- Music: HEY _____

- Film: THE ITALIAN _____

- Drama: FRIENDS, _____, COUNTRYMEN

- Literature: _____ DEFOE

- Language: QUESTION _____

- Sport: BABE _____

- Mathematics: IMAGINARY _____

14. Plus This

I follow B on the wrist, and H at the end of it; after L I'm
solid ground, and S at the edge of it. I join couples together,
but when I follow R as an author, what's my three-letter first
name?

15. Kropki

Place a number from 1 to 8 into each square, so that each number appears once per row and column.

1	2	4	3	5
4	1	2	5	3
5	4	3	2	1
2	3	5	1	4
3	5	1	4	2

A white dot between two squares indicates that the values in those squares are consecutive (i.e. have a difference of 1); a black dot indicates that the value in one square is twice that in the other. All possible dots are given, except for between 1 and 2 in which case just one of the possible dots is given. An example solution for 1 to 5 is given.

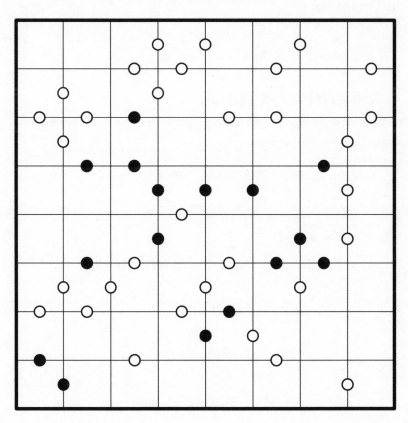

16. In a Sorry State

Can you unscramble the following themed anagrams and then determine what entry could come next in this ordered list?

- LONGED

- BAREVE

- REVENGERE

- MEG

- AUSTERER

- ACEEP DANGER

17. Sounds Familiar

Can you use the following definitions to reach a one-word answer?

- _____: spherical green seed

- _____: second person

- _____: 'be', in the present tense plural

- _____: organ of sight

- _____: hot drink made from leaves

- _____: for what reason?

18. Follow the Rule

What comes next in the following sequence?

- A
- G1
- G2
- G3
- G4
- W4
- V
- E7
- G5
- E8
- G6

19. Liquid Vowels

All of the vowels in the following alcoholic spirits have been consumed. What were the original spirits?

- TQL
- RMGNC
- Z
- SMBC
- RM
- BSNTH

20. Increasing Sudoku

Place 1 to 9 once each into every row, column and bold-lined 3×3 box of this puzzle.

Numbers along any grey line must increase in value from one end to the other, such as for example 2 4 5 7 9. A number cannot repeat on a grey line.

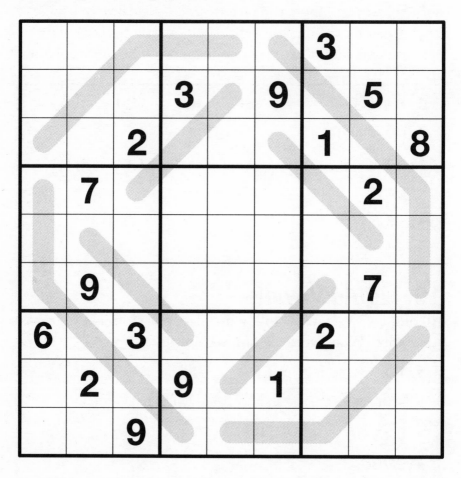

21. Bridges

The following diagram represents an array of islands which you must join together with bridges, so that you can travel from any island to any other island simply by crossing over one or more bridges.

Each island must be connected by as many bridges as is shown on it, and there can be either zero, one or two bridges between any pair of islands. Bridges must be horizontal or vertical, and cannot cross over either each other or an island.

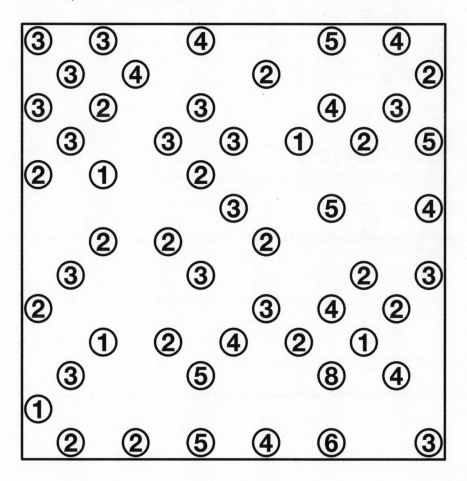

22. Flower Arranging

Place these words into order, from longest to shortest. Length is defined according to a criterion which it is your job to discern.

- HERON
- HOUNDS
- LINE
- ORIEL
- REIGN
- ROAN
- SHIRTY

23. Six Notes

What do all of the following have in common?

- Not fastened
- Long-term employment
- Giving a title to
- Expedition to observe or hunt animals
- Soak up
- Highly seasoned sausage
- Use of irony to expose stupidity

24. Numbers Games

All of these cities have had their years removed. What would be the next entry in this sequence?

- ODEANEIRO
- NDON
- BIJING
- AHNS
- SDNEY
- TLANA

- _____

25. Showing Off

Which TV shows are these?

- → FRI ←

- BRINK AGE

- ♠ ♥ ♦ ♣

-      ONCE
  THREE O'CLOCK

- S S S CO.

26. The Great Pyramid

The answer to each of the following clues contains the same letters as the previous word, plus one extra, albeit possibly in a jumbled order. What are each of the words?

- Sculpture, perhaps
- Shopping receptacle
- Faint remains, perhaps
- Sugary fluid
- Takes it back, in a way
- Does it again
- Appearances on stage
- Certain fruits
- Burns to ashes
- Bequeathments

27. Publication Puzzle

Fitzwilliam College produces three publications: *The Billy Bulletin*, *The Goat Post*, and *Optima*. One is published annually, one termly and one weekly. One is only read by undergraduates, one by all students, and one by all students and staff.

The following facts are also all true:

- *The Goat Post* has a bigger readership than the weekly publication.

- The publication that is read by all students but not staff is produced more frequently than *Optima*.

- The publication that is only read by undergraduates has a title that references the college's mascot: the billy goat.

Given this information, can you deduce the readership of each publication and how frequently each is produced?

28. Firsts and Lasts

Can you form each given number of words by adding the same letter to the start and the end of each of these partial words?

For example, __ON__ can be used to form two words by adding either an S or a G, to make SONS or GONG.

- 2 words: __ ORT __
- 7 words: __ U __
- 4 words: __ EA __
- 3 words: __ UL __
- 3 words: __ ASHE __
- 3 words: __ EE __
- 3 words: __ RO __
- 6 words: __ I __
- 2 words: __ OLLE __

29. Diagonal Number Link

Draw a set of paths to link each pair of identical numbers. Paths can run horizontally, vertically or diagonally between squares, but only one path can enter any square.

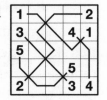

Paths *can* cross, but only diagonally at the intersection of four squares. A solved example is shown.

Try this puzzle first:

1				2	3
4				5	
		5			
				3	2
		4			1
6	7		6		7

Now try this wider puzzle:

1				2	3	4	5
6			6				3
		2					4
1	7	8	7		8		5

30. Sum Skyscraper

Place a number from 1 to 6 into each row and column within the grid of this skyscraper puzzle. These numbers represent skyscrapers of between 1 and 6 floors respectively.

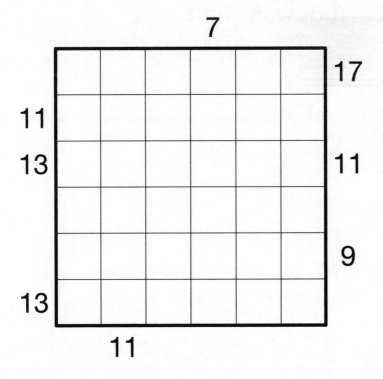

Clue numbers at one end of a row or column give the *total* number of floors of the <u>visible</u> skyscrapers that can be seen from that point.

A skyscraper is <u>visible</u> if no taller skyscraper precedes it in the same row or column, reading from the direction of the clue. In the example, the '16' on the left gives the total of the 1, 4, 5 and 6 skyscrapers, with the 2 and 3 being hidden.

31. Tone Deafness

Unscramble the following anagrams and then determine the way in which they might be considered 'tone-deaf'.

- ABASHTB

- AYD

- FOLDY

- RABRY

- SEMJA

- STOREY TULC

- THO HILIC PERPESP

32. Worldwide Tour

The name of which country can be written without using any letters that appear in the names of any of the countries listed below?

- CAPE VERDE

- CHAD

- KYRGYZSTAN

- LUXEMBOURG

- NEW ZEALAND

- QATAR

33. Salad Days

The following five two-word clues hint at five different items in a particular category, and do so in five different ways as shown. Can you solve the clues and identify the category?

- Barrier Boy
- Woman Stop
- Moose Merry
- Coat Rip
- Lie Chi

Methods of hint:

- Anagram
- Antonyms
- Homophone
- Rhyme
- Synonyms

34. What's That?

What is notable about the following phrases?

- Collaborate together
- Downward descent
- Exact replica
- First conceived
- Unexpected surprise

35. Facing Off

The face is missing from one of these three cubes. Which of the faces listed beneath should replace the blank face, so that all three views could then be showing the same cube?

The possible faces are:

36. Word Search

Can you find all of these listed entries in the grid? They are all written in a straight line, in any direction.

```
N  A  1  S  R  F  O  O  2  R  K  6  D  I  A
2  N  E  M  E  S  I  W  3  D  1  1  W  F  0
O  V  E  R  W  8  N  0  L  T  D  1  E  V  W
0  S  K  R  2  R  A  R  E  R  2  M  E  I  R
2  M  A  E  W  1  2  E  R  T  I  R  2  U  T
R  X  C  C  D  N  W  D  H  9  1  1  S  E  0
E  O  O  4  E  S  C  7  E  0  F  U  8  D  1
D  W  A  I  S  T  K  N  0  S  N  R  L  1  S
N  I  C  1  R  A  1  0  1  9  E  O  8  I  I
U  N  L  K  E  4  0  0  S  V  F  S  E  S  X
A  C  0  R  4  0  0  S  E  0  R  1  1  0  0
D  1  B  E  0  W  O  2  0  E  I  L  T  1  N
E  E  D  0  8  L  R  0  I  I  5  E  K  A  T
9  A  D  0  W  D  1  4  1  E  9  A  C  A  1
8  I  2  S  B  C  O  N  D  I  T  I  1  R  W
```

- ACETONE
- ADENINE
- ANCIENT WORLD
- ART WORK
- BREAKS EVEN
- CANINE
- CLONE
- CONDITIONER
- DOZENTH
- ELEVENSES
- ENGROSSED
- FEMININE
- FOOTWORK
- FOURIER
- FREIGHT
- HUNDREDWEIGHT
- NON-EXISTENT
- OVERWEIGHT
- SUNNINESS
- SWEET SIXTEEN
- TAKE FIVE
- TENSIONED
- THOUSANDFOLD
- THREE WISE MEN
- UNDERSCORE
- VERMILLION

37. Movie Match-Up

Can you match up the two halves of these movie titles, each of which have an 'on' in between them?

All Quiet		34th Street
Angel		A Hot Tin Roof
A Nightmare		A Plane
Bird		A Scandal
Born		A Train
Breakfast		A Wire
Cat		Cedars
Death		Earth
Fiddler	*on*	Elm Street
Lean		Me
Man		My Shoulder
Miracle		Pluto
Mutiny		The Bounty
Notes		The Fourth of July
Snakes		The Moon
Snow Falling		The Nile
Strangers		The River Kwai
The Bridge		The Roof
The Greatest Show		The Verge of a Nervous Breakdown
Women		The Western Front

38. Spiral Crossword

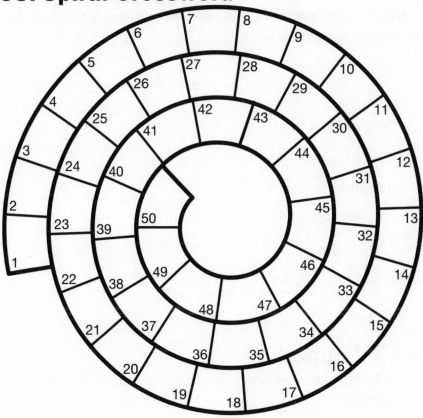

Inward

1-6   Encumbrance
7-10   Chooses, with 'for'
11-17 Gap
18-20 Nada
21-25 Built-up
26-32 Submerged in water
33-37 Reasoning
38-42 Propose
43-50 Moved through a
        digital document

Outward

50-47 Wooded valley
46-43 War-loving fantasy
        creatures
42-40 Umpire
39-36 Central points
35-30 Gilt
29-26 Linguistic unit
25-23 Seize
22-17 Governing
16-13 Three squared
12-5   Defer
4-1   Thoroughly defeat

39. Characterful Writing

Sort these words and phrases into two groups, according to their inner characters.

- Crème anglais

- Demeanour

- Humankind

- Kindergarten

- Meander

- Ramekin dish

- Skin-deep

- Time and again

40. TV Schedule

There are three television shows that are original to a local channel:

- A Farm in the City

- Silence is Golden

- They Wouldn't Dare

One has run for one season, one for two seasons, and one for three seasons. One has 20-minute episodes, one has 40-minute episodes, and one has one-hour episodes.

The following facts are also true:
- 'They Wouldn't Dare' has shorter episodes than the show that has only run for one season.

- The show that has only run for two seasons is earlier in the alphabet than the one with 20-minute episodes.

- The show with one-hour episodes has fewer seasons than 'Silence is Golden'.

Based on this information, can you deduce how many seasons each show has run for, and the length of each show's episodes?

41. One Stair at a Time

To make it safely to the next floor I must take it one stair at a time. Make sense of my musings below and tell me – will I make it?

Reading the first 'epistle' from my sister, now a politician, wasn't easy. There was a moment when I thought of throwing it in the waste paper basket. It was my stepbrother who finally helped me. He made me a mug of his tepid tea – a family special. The familiar taste promptly cheered me up. He told me that his friend, Stephen, had had a similar problem. Reading political pamphlets is an acquired taste, perhaps. I gave up reading and decided to cut and paste paragraphs to make my own version instead. This would be a much better version for her to take doorstepping!

42. A Worthy Puzzle

Group these words into triplets:

- Hyena
- Propounding
- Neuron
- Cayenne
- European
- Doyen
- Impound
- Pleuron
- Compound

43. Focal Words

What connects the words that are clued by the following?

- Flat
- Turned into a god
- Female school teacher
- Data and numbers in general
- More crimson
- Individual performances
- Sneaky look
- Helicopter blade
- Type of canoe

44. Equal Division

Draw along some of the lines in this image in order to divide it into four identical shapes. Shapes are still considered identical if they are rotated relative to one another, but not if they are reflected.

All of the existing image must be used – none of the squares may be left over.

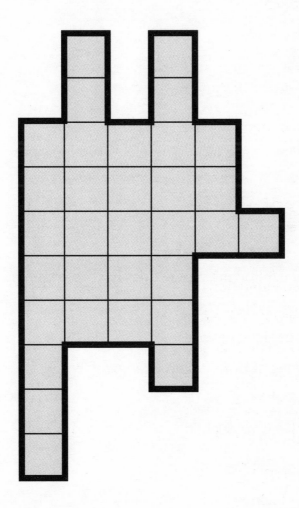

45. TV Introductions

Which television show does each of these sets of initials represent?

- HIMYM
- OITNB
- TAAHM
- SATC
- GOT
- TBBT
- TFPOB-A
- TTZ
- STTNG
- BTVS

46. A Shark's Tale

What do the following movie titles have in common?

- The Da Vinci Code
- Shakespeare in Love
- A Series of Unfortunate Events
- The Ambassador
- A Brilliant Young Mind
- Man of Steel

47. Drink Dilemma

The three drinks available at a particular bar are Crocodile's Cool Cider, Regal Lager and Femmefat Ale. One drink is 4.5% alcohol, one is 5% and the third is 6%. One is from Australia, one is from Belgium, and the third is from the UK.

- Crocodile's Cool Cider is weaker than the Belgian beer.

- The Australian beer has a longer name than the 4.5% beer.

- Regal Lager is from an English-speaking country.

Based on this information, can you deduce the nationality and percentage of each beer?

48. Cheesy Story

Can you quantify the cheesiness of this tale?

We were staying in a battle-damaged baroque fortress for the week. I put on bleached dark jeans and a taffeta blouse and went downstairs to cook an apricot tart. I began by putting fruit in a pan. Eerily, the cooking pots were clattering. It made the pans tilt one way and then the other, here in Monterey. Jack, my partner, heard nothing and dismissed my fears. He called them mental images, and my ordinary par. Me, sane?!

49. Number Darts

Can you pick one number from each ring of this unusual dartboard in order to make each of the given totals?

Numbers can be used again across totals, but only one number per ring may be used for any individual total.

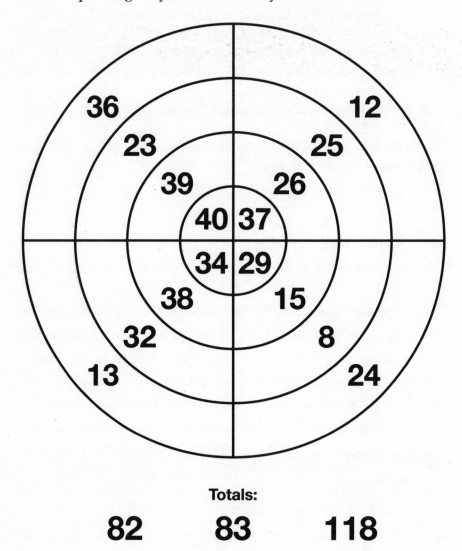

Totals:

82   **83**   **118**

50. Wet Room

In what way can these words and phrases all be said to clue something that is wet?

- Refuse to give something that is due to another

- A building for keeping a carriage

- A provider of cheap accommodation for young people

- A bent piece of metal that has bait attached

- Boisterous or violent behaviour

- A former name for Belize

51. Aesthetic Connection

What connects all of the following words?

- Column

- Answer

- Gnome

- Indict

- Thumb

- Aisle

- Autumn

- Leopard

- Psychology

52. One Direction
Which way haven't these words gone?

- UNORTHODOX

- BEASTLY

- AWESTRUCK

53. One Connection
What links these words?

- OVERSTOCK

- DEFACE

- SOMNOLENCE

- STUBBORN

- HYDROXYZINE

- ECDEMIC

Chapter 4
Enigmas

1. Mixed Signals

You are a spy, and a very important code word has been transmitted to you. However, your equipment is faulty, and you end up receiving the following nonsensical words:

- BARLEY
- MOTEL
- CUNEIFORM
- GNARLY
- FILO
- SCHEMA
- GECKO
- SHELTER

Can you work out what's gone wrong with the message, and find the code word?

2. Take It Up a Notch

Can you match the definitions on the left with their pairs on the right that have all been shifted up a gear?

Bestow (4)	Appear (4)
Choose (4)	Become happier (5)
Circle (4)	Become immobile (5)
Create (4)	Begin to cry (4)
Cut shorter (4)	Be obsequious (4)
Draw into the mouth (4)	Call by phone (4)
Exhale rapidly (4)	Cheers (7)
Fissure (5)	Collect (4)
Grab (5)	Confess (3)
Perform a role (3)	Explode (4)
Possess (3)	Misbehave (3)
Project (5)	Reconcile (4)
Rear (4)	Regurgitate (5)
Rears (7)	Reverse (4)
Receive (3)	Rise (3)
Rest (5)	Separate (5)
Shellfish (4)	Speak out (4)
Shout in support (5)	Start laughing (5)
Tube (4)	Stop talking (4)
Water source (4)	Surrender (4)

3. State of the Art

Can you map the gaps to reveal a US state?

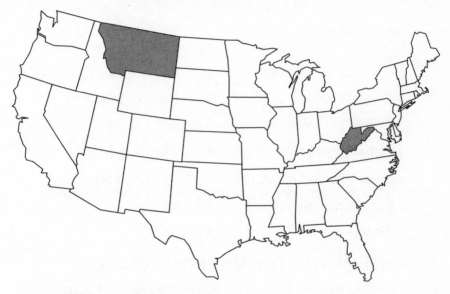

- Liquor: _ _ C _ _ _ O L
- Making sure: A _ _ E R T A I _ _ E N T
- Insect: _ _ T E R P _ _ L A R
- Prohibiting: F _ _ B _ _ _ D I N G
- Dangerous: H _ _ _ _ _ D O U S
- With one spouse: _ _ N O _ _ M O U S
- Pervasiveness: P R E _ _ L E _ _ E
- Wiry: S _ _ E _ _ _
- Tents: W I G _ _ _ _ _

4. Period Drama

Five novelists have been broken down in some way and then added together again to obtain the following results:

- AUSTEN = 154

- BRONTE = 102

- HARDY = 85

- LAWRENCE = 271

- STEINBECK = 146 *or* 157

Using the same process, what is the value of KEROUAC?

5. Arithmetic for Vexillologists

Can you earn your stripes by completing the final sum?

Lithuania	Switzerland	Poland	=	5
Nigeria	Jamaica	Guinea	=	9
Canada	Dominica	Barbados	=	6
Thailand	Georgia	Tajikistan	=	___

6. Wraparound Sudoku

Place 1 to 9 once each into every row, column and jigsaw-shaped region of this fiendish sudoku puzzle.

All but one of the jigsaw-shaped regions wrap around the edges of the puzzle. A region that does not contain a bold border at the edge of the puzzle 'wraps around' and continues at the opposite end of that row or column.

	5		3	4		6		
					3			5
5								
	9							6
8								3
7							5	
								8
3			2					
		7		9	8		2	

7. Roman Emperors

Can you identify the missing number?

- Claudius = 651

- Galba = 50

- Vitellius = 107

- Titus = 1

- Domitian = 1502

- Nerva = _____

8. Common Bond

What comes next in the following sequence?

- S

- S

- QOS

- CR

- DAD

- TWINE

- TND

- G

- LTK

9. Novel Presentations

What novel do each of the following represent?

- THERYTHECATCHERE

- DANIELLE RUBY ZOE
  → JANE SARAH ELIZABETH ←

- BRAVE DR LOW

- MARCH → MARCH ← MARCH

- REVILO

- 232.8°C

- ROAD
  THE

- BOMENMENMENAT

- THE SNOOZE

- @
  EMENT

10. Not Needed

Something has been added to this word search puzzle. What?

Y	R	N	E	U	S	S	U	R	R	P	L	U	S	O
R	I	L	R	I	N	D	E	P	E	L	E	A	T	D
A	U	N	N	S	E	E	D	E	D	T	M	N	R	R
I	D	D	R	D	E	S	H	N	R	A	A	E	E	A
L	E	Y	Y	T	L	D	F	A	R	D	X	T	T	A
I	E	R	I	R	L	S	P	U	E	O	S	N	T	E
T	D	A	O	X	E	S	Y	N	A	E	L	L	F	L
X	D	L	U	E	R	A	U	L	R	R	A	N	Y	L
U	A	L	E	I	R	D	I	V	E	E	T	L	E	S
A	E	I	R	S	E	X	E	D	T	L	E	H	D	V
S	S	C	L	R	S	A	C	C	I	B	I	C	E	N
E	A	X	O	Y	T	E	E	E	U	S	D	A	U	R
S	R	N	M	E	C	E	V	L	S	I	B	C	L	S
V	Y	A	N	U	R	U	T	E	U	S	I	U	C	E
E	S	H	T	A	S	P	A	D	E	M	E	R	S	E

- ADDED
- ANCILLARY
- AUXILIARY
- EXCESS
- FURTHER
- MORE
- REDUNDANT
- RESERVE
- SPARE
- SUBSIDIARY
- SURPLUS
- UNNEEDED

11. Daily Presenting

Which fictional presenter might come next in this list?

- Swimming Pool

- Canada Geese

- Gold Dust

- Calling Card

- French Horn

- Snapping Turtle

12. Medals Table

A country's medals table by sport for the Olympics is shown below. Can you fill in the missing line?

Sport	G	S	B
Artistic Gymnastics	1	3	0
Basketball	0	1	2
Dressage	1	2	0
Greco-Roman Wrestling	2	1	0
Swimming	1	1	0
Weightlifting	___	___	___

13. Increasing Complexity

Solve each of the following clues. The solutions form a
particular sequence.

- Mouser
- Hypocrisy
- Perform
- Semi-conscious state
- Particular
- Respond to one another
- Elaborate
- Monologue, perhaps
- Reciprocal influence
- Brainwash

14. Nothing in Common?

What do the following capital cities have in common?

- Cairo
- Lima
- Montevideo
- Rome
- Suva
- Tokyo
- Vaduz

15. Heirs and Graces

Who doesn't belong?

- Code Liar
- One Girl
- Anger
- Halo Pie
- Rain Mad
- Raged
- To Pair
- Done Dames

16. Don't Look!

What should you do instead?

	O	O		O		O	O	O
O	O		O				O	O
O		O		O	O			

17. What am I?

I turn the remains of a wound red, and I can get one of three babies from a single journey. After certain meat I turn into a Shakespearean prince, and yet I'm half a character.

I will permit you to rent, so what am I?

18. Dashing Around

Can you put
Morse code
Into words to
Solve
This dotty puzzle
And therefore
Answer this: Dashing around,
Which way up?

19. Doubling Down

What bird is missing from this list?

- Brethren

- Minimized

- Fanfare

- Lysosome

- Balaclava

- Activation

20. Off the Rails

A train has come off both of its rails and crashed into the fence! The driver has managed to communicate the following message. Can you figure out where it's gone?

ISTXODICSTAOFRCRU

21. Making Waves

What single six-letter word could a sailor use to communicate the dates of all of these battles, in the order listed?

- The Battle of Trnava

- The Siege of Galle

- The Battle of Taejon

- The Decembrist Revolt

- The Battle of Sari Bair

- The Chittagong Armoury Raid

22. Triple Triplets

Solve these nine clues and join the resulting answers into three sets, each of three words. Each of these three sets shares two related properties. A further property connects all nine answers.

- Travelled in a hurry

- Less well-considered

- Wearable ranking ribbons

- Made a noise like a bell

- Athletic substitute

- Slightly burns

- No longer on this mortal coil

- Raise on the hind legs

- Marine regions

23. Movie Match-Up

Can you match up the two halves of these movie titles, each of which have an 'of' in between them?

A Fistful		Africa
A History		A Murder
Anatomy		Arabia
Bridge		Dollars
Children		Frankenstein
City		God
Dawn		Horrors
Eternal Sunshine		Men
Invasion	*of*	Music
Lawrence		Others
Little Shop		Our Lives
Out		Oz
The Best Years		Spies
The Bride		The Body Snatchers
The Grapes		The Dead
The Lives		The Sierra Madre
The Silence		The Spotless Mind
The Sound		The Lambs
The Treasure		Violence
The Wizard		Wrath

24. Dice Decision

You have the following shape net:

If you were to cut this out and fold it up to make a cube, which of the following would result?

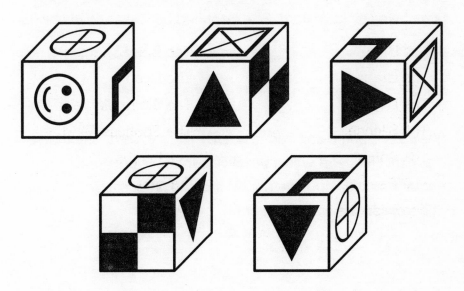

25. Grey Matter

The following song titles have each had one word replaced with a synonym. What are the original titles of the songs, and what is the theme linking these changes?

- Ash on the Water

- When Flints Cry

- Maxwell's Charcoal Hammer

- Bennie and the Clouds

26. Enlightened

One of these sentences in this tale of woe is so much darker than the rest. Which one?

In spite of lamentable circumstances, she kept on going – gardening kept her calm. But she felt so misunderstood by him. It was flight or fight. She clenched her fists and clamped her lips shut.

But then, she saw him enter the garden.

She seized some soil from a nearby planter; next, she threw it at him. Her heart was ablaze! She took his precious, fragrant orchids and she ripped them to shreds, right in front of his eyes. She was full of fire.

27. Flying Friends

Find all of these birds in the word search.

```
P O N L L A L T B R R P N A B
A C R I R L L U I W N A G B T
H S A K F N N O B T L I L O I
I H T F U I N C C W N K B K R
C I K D F H L I H K A I H K U
C F T I A I R K K U N H C H R
R B P P P R T O R R I I O H N
F E S K N U E K W G L A R E L
K N T E U I Y W A E T B I A R
E I A E Y L S W R R D C C L W
T R P L L K B C C A R K K A V
K H A H B K S G W L L E N A J
G B G W T A N K A I N L V V R
R I W I L I C W B L R A I I G
N A R B C W L K I L E D L N T
```

- BLACKBIRD
- BLUE TIT
- BULLFINCH
- CHAFFINCH
- DUNNOCK
- JACKDAW
- NIGHTINGALE
- PIPIT
- RAVEN
- ROBIN
- SKYLARK
- SPARROW
- TITLARK
- WAGTAIL
- WARBLER

28. Holed Calcudoku

Place 1 to 8 once each into every row and column.

Each bold-lined region must result in the value given at its top-left when the operation given in the same location is applied between all of the numbers in that region.

For subtraction and division, start with the largest number in the region and subtract or divide by the remaining numbers in the region.

12+		48×	6×	24×	140×		
	280×						6−
60×		24×				17+	
							18×
	96×					13+	
5+							
				42×	8+		1−
48×							

29. Feeling Tense

Pair these words, based on the words they conceal.

- Aftershave
- Aniseed
- Ashiness
- Chainsaw
- Crunch
- Cultivate
- Dishonest
- Eyeshadow
- Meatball
- Transport

30. Novel Introductions

Which famous novels do these initials stand for?

- OHYOS by GGM
- TBJ by SP
- TCOMC by AD
- TCP by AW
- TKAM by HL
- TPODG by OW

31. Written Problem

What is special about the words clued by the following?

- Light, lettuce-based meals

- Containers for liquids

- Starts to tire

- Sudden, bright light

- Window material

- Certain volcano deposits

- A US state

32. Connection Question

Can you pair up these words?

- COUNTRIES

- TRIANGLES

- NEUROTICS

- RESIDENTS

- GREATNESS

- GNARLIEST

- EMIGRANTS

- TIREDNESS

- STREAMING

- SERGEANTS

33. More Number Darts

Can you pick one number from each ring of this unusual dartboard in order to make each of the given totals?

Numbers can be used again across totals, but only one number per ring may be used for any individual total.

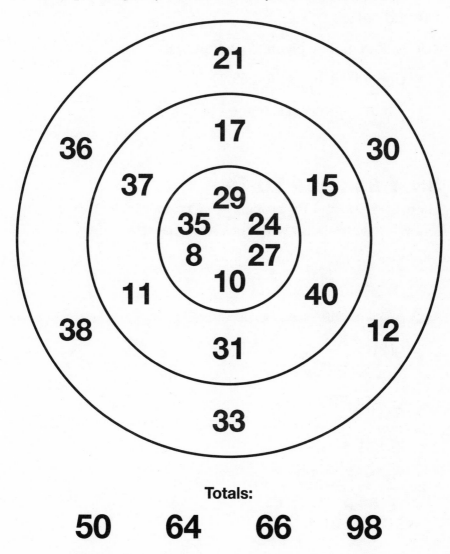

Totals:

50   64   66   98

34. Add Homonym

Each of the following entries audibly clues a two-word phrase. Can you identify each of the phrases?

- Hole-piercing tool tavern

- Caught sight of pimple

- Lid defect

- Naked money given to poor people

- Upper limit strikes forcefully

- Pitched watery discharge from the eyes

35. Back and Forth

There is an interesting property that connects all of the following words. Can you work out what it is?

- SANCTION

- OVERSIGHT

- BOUND

- DUST

- LEFT

- RESIGN

- SCREEN

- TRANSPARENT

- TEMPER

36. Further Equal Division

Draw along some of the lines in this image in order to divide it into four identical shapes. Shapes are still considered identical if they are rotated relative to one another, but not if they are reflected.

All of the existing image must be used – none of the squares may be left over.

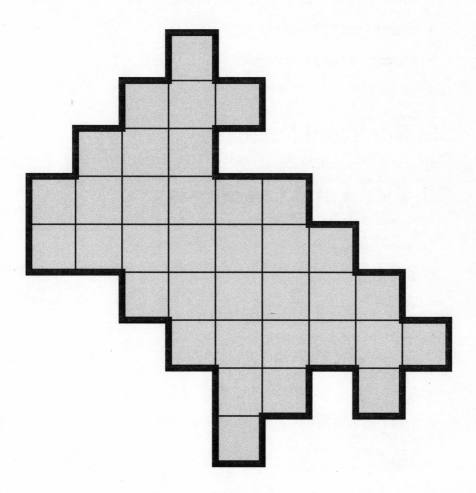

37. Word Twins

The following words can be formed into duos. Can you work out the pairs?

- Cruise
- Fox
- Fry
- Hardy
- Merchant
- Pine
- Rock
- Sheen

38. Elemental Chemicals

What is special about all of the following elements?

- Phosphorus
- Silicon
- Iron
- Tin
- Arsenic
- Bismuth
- Xenon
- Neon

39. Just a Second

What comes next in each of the following sequences?

- N, W, H, O, I, I, __

- A, E, A, P, A, U, __

- O, U, E, H, R, A, __

- E, R, E, R, L, N, __

40. Double Negatives

Am I feeling positive – or not?

'Another year, another me,' I said to myself. 'And this year I'm not going to make the same mistakes as last year.'

I began to annotate my notebooks from the previous year. At first, the task was quite hypnotic. After a while, however, knots began to form in my stomach, which always denotes trouble.

Every year has become so monotonous. Notionally, I'm changing, but I now see it is not really the case. There's no domino theory here.

I poured myself a glass of Pinot and let my belt out a notch. I had barely noticed the year passing. My notoriety had increased, but what had I really gained?

'Another year, another me,' I said to myself. 'Or not!'

41. Common Parts

What do the following definitions have in common?

- To consume without feeling sick

- To pay, as in the bill

- To pick something up and give it to someone

- To provide with weapons

- To tease good-naturedly

- To look at with interest

42. Double Concealment

Can you pair up these words, based on components of each?

- Ballet

- Batches

- Cleft

- Clock

- Frighten

- Impeaches

- Jockey

- Minute

- Selfish

- Screaming

- Thunderbolt

- Woodchips

43. Blod Broothers

The table below has been constructed from pairs of words that contain the same sound but have that sound spelled differently. Then, the spellings of the sounds have been swapped within each pair. Can you match up each word on the left with its pair on the right?

Blud	Acshun
Boughin	Coff
Deight	Crood
Feald	Foon
Feand	Frate
Ligher	Hiar
Mude	Miel
Pough	Miet
Poughst	Tho
Tiot	Tuff

44. Foreign Films

Can you identify what has happened to the following movie titles?

- A Passage to When Idle
- Big Trouble in Little Gin Jibe
- Good Morning, Ha Ion
- The Boys from Bias Liar
- The Prince of Oi Car

45. Minesweeper Message

What message is this minesweeper puzzle hiding? Find out by shading in all of the hidden mines.

Numbers in the grid reveal the number of mines in the surrounding eight squares *plus* the square itself, i.e. nine squares in total – so you can shade the numbered squares as well as the white squares. Clues still apply, even if shaded.

					2		4	3			
	5	4	4		5				7	5	
	3						6			2	
	3				5		4		5	7	
		2	2			2			3	3	
2								3		5		4
			3	3	3				3	3	2
4	6	4			5	5	4		5	5	
		4	6			5		4			2
4			6	3				3	5	5	
2		2	4		2		2	3		3	
				2				4		6	2
					4	3	3	3			2
	4	1			6		5		5	7	
				3		4			4	6	4
		5	4	3					4	6	4
	2		2		2		3	3		3	

46. Word Report

Can you pair up the following according to a common rule?

- Allow
- Become narrower
- Call into question
- Competition
- Decline
- Explanation of behaviour
- Forgive
- Formal agreement
- Make a complaint
- Manner of behaviour
- Official certificate
- Property or quality
- Proposal
- Regard as belonging to
- Throw forwards
- Tangible thing
- Transmit heat
- Waste

47. Wrap-around Number Link

Draw a set of paths to link each pair of identical numbers. Paths can run horizontally or vertically between squares, but only one path can enter any square. Paths cannot touch or cross.

Paths can continue off one edge of the grid and then 'wrap around' to continue on the opposite end of the same row or column. A small solved example is shown.

And now try this even-tougher puzzle:

48. In and Out

Solve each of the following clues. The answer to every clue is connected to both the preceding and following answers.

- Disappointments
- Choppers?
- Was overcome with admiration
- Bequeaths property, perhaps
- Planted seed
- Causes of distress
- Be in the red
- Had on
- Not as good
- Cleansing process?
- More sparkly, perhaps
- Local somebodies
- In a different way

49. Take It Away

What is so great that you can take it away from this puzzle?

- Overlaid
- Large grocery store
- A-lister
- Invigilator

50. Cryptic Connection

Each of these three entries clues a member of the same set. What does each entry refer to, and what is that set?

- e.g.1:0 p (have debt)

- H_2O about you+me

- π observes

51. Friendly Names

Can you join the following names into pairs, according to a certain rule? One name will be left over.

- ADAM
- ALASTAIR
- ANASTASIA
- ANGELA
- ANNABEL
- CARMEN
- CHAD
- DUNCAN
- IAN
- ILENE
- KEN
- LEIGH

- MENA

- MITCH

- OSBORNE

- PANSY

- SKYE

- SONJA

- YASMINE

52. Double Down

By doubling down as you solve these clues, can you reveal what you now are?

- Indian bread's grandmother

- Ringer sound level

- Punctuation's unresponsive state

- Kind deity

- Moved busily and joined together

- Resentful animal that needs a muzzle?

- Offering a price and waiting for a good opportunity

- Original decay

- Aimed and smoothed flat

- Unwanted plant tied a knot?

53. Final Bite

Can you reveal every bit of this final message?

				1		1		
				2	1	1	2	
		1		1	3	1	2	
		1		2	4	1	2	
		3		1	2	1	4	

A nonogram grid with the following row clues (top to bottom): 1,1 · 1 · 1,1 · 5 · 2 · 1 · 1,2 · 1,1 · 5 · 1,1 · 3 · 1,1 · 3 · 2,1 · 1

Solutions 1:
Amusements

1. Linked Anagrams

The words are:

- BOARD
- FACE
- END
- MIND
- CARD

- FAIR
- BIG
- THEORY
- PLAN
- BOY

The common theme is 'GAME', since this can be prefixed either before or after each word to make either a new word or a phrase.

2. Twenty or Less

The words are:

- EIGHTEEN
- ELEVEN
- FIFTEEN
- FIVE
- FOUR
- NINE

- ONE
- SEVEN
- SIX
- TEN
- THIRTEEN
- THREE

- TWELVE
- TWENTY
- TWO
- ZERO

3. Newly Named Novels

- *Gone with the Wind*
- *The Grapes of Wrath*
- *War and Peace*
- *Brave New World*
- *Animal Farm*
- *The Scarlet Letter*
- *Crime and Punishment*
- *The Catcher in Rye*
- *A Farewell to Arms*
- *Great Expectations*
- *White Teeth*

4. Speaking in Circles

A ring.

5. Square Loop

6. Black-out Sudoku

4		5	8	6	1	3	2	7
9	6	3	5	2		1	4	8
2	1	7	9	3	4		6	5
	4	6	1	7	5	8	9	3
1	7	2	3		8	6	5	4
8	5	9	6	4	2	7	1	
6	8	1	7	5	3	4		2
7	2	4		1	9	5	3	6
5	3		2	8	6	9	7	1

7. Movie Match-Up

An Officer	and	A Gentleman
Antony		Cleopatra
Beauty		The Beast
Bonnie		Clyde
Butch Cassidy		The Sundance Kid
Dazed		Confused

Dumb		Dumber
Four Weddings		A Funeral
Guys		Dolls
Hannah	and	Her Sisters
Harold		Maude
Monty Python		The Holy Grail
Planes, Trains		Automobiles
Rosencrantz		Guildenstern are Dead
Sense		Sensibility
Sex, Lies		Videotape
The Diving Bell		The Butterfly
The Good, the Bad		The Ugly
Thelma		Louise
Withnail		I

8. Presidential Mix-Up

The anagrams are:

- WILSON + E
- ADAMS + H
- JACKSON + E
- CLEVELAND + I
- HAYES + N
- GARFIELD + S
- FILLMORE + O
- COOLIDGE + E
- WASHINGTON + R
- ROOSEVELT + W

The extra letters are an anagram of EISENHOWER.

9. What Can You Do?

These are all things you can break, as in you can break a fall, break a habit, break a leg, and so on.

10. Daisy Chain

DAISY	
SANDY	light yellowish-brown
STAND	be on one's feet
WANTS	desires
STRAW	dried stalks of grain
TRAPS	snares
DARTS	small pointed missiles
SHARD	piece of broken glass
SHADY	out of the sun
DAISY	

11. What the Dickens?

- OLIVER TWIST
- DAVID COPPERFIELD
- EBENEZER SCROOGE
- MISS HAVISHAM
- NICHOLAS NICKLEBY
- MARTIN CHUZZLEWIT
- ABEL MAGWITCH
- FAGIN
- BARNABY RUDGE
- SYDNEY CARTON

12. Back for Seconds

There must have been 30 slices to start with.

13. Literary Logic

Across the Lake is a detective novel written by Walker. *One Hundred Degrees* is a science fiction novel written by Davies. *One Long Night* is a romance novel written by Carter.

14. Dangerous Music

The blanks are:

- EARTH
- SONG
- BEN
- BEAT
- IT
- BAD
- BLACK
- OR
- WHITE

Reading down the list are five song titles: *Earth Song, Ben, Beat It, Bad* and *Black or White*. These are all Michael Jackson songs.

15. Mixed Pictures

The anagrams are:

- ACHORUS = CRASH + O,U
- ACTINGFIT = TITANIC + F,G
- HANDRING = GANDHI + N,R
- LATEADORING = GLADIATOR + E,N

- SUAVEMAID = AMADEUS + I,V

The extra letters are an anagram of UNFORGIVEN.

16. Dotty Loop

17. Arrow Sudoku

1	5	6	2	4	8	3	9	7
4	7	3	5	1	9	6	8	2
9	2	8	3	7	6	4	1	5
7	6	2	4	9	3	8	5	1
5	4	1	6	8	7	2	3	9
3	8	9	1	5	2	7	6	4
8	1	5	7	6	4	9	2	3
6	3	4	9	2	5	1	7	8
2	9	7	8	3	1	5	4	6

18. Pyramidal

- ACT
- CHAT
- TEACH
- CHASTE

- ARCHEST
- STANCHER
- MERCHANTS
- PARCHMENTS

19. Fab Forewords

The unscrambled words are:

- ELEANOR
- PAPERBACK
- RIGBY
- SUBMARINE
- JUDE
- TOGETHER
- BACK

- YELLOW
- COME
- LANE
- PENNY
- GET
- WRITER
- HEY

Paired up, these make up the titles of Beatles songs: *Come Together, Eleanor Rigby, Get Back, Hey Jude, Paperback Writer, Penny Lane, and Yellow Submarine.*

20. Easy as a Sequence

The sequence is the digits of Pi after the decimal point, i.e. 3.1415926, and so the next number is 5 since the next digit in Pi would be 5, since Pi to eight decimal places is 3.14159265.

21. A Leg to Stand On

13 of the guests are dogs (and 17 are humans).

22. Wordoku

The hidden word is 'PASSWORDS'.

P	E	R	W	S	D	T	O	A
W	A	D	O	P	T	E	S	R
O	T	S	R	E	A	P	W	D
D	O	W	S	R	P	A	T	E
S	P	A	T	W	E	D	R	O
T	R	E	A	D	O	S	P	W
A	W	P	D	O	S	R	E	T
R	S	T	E	A	W	O	D	P
E	D	O	P	T	R	W	A	S

23. Reckoning by the Rules

Rule A = flower names; Rule B = five-letter girl's names

Rule A	Rule B	Rules A and B	Neither A nor B
ORCHID	GRACE	POPPY	JANE
VIOLET	SALLY	DAISY	PLUM
AZALEA	FLEUR	ERICA	PEAR
PINK	ALICE	TANSY	MIRANDA
CLOVER	**ELLEN**		**SHARON**
IRIS			

24. Word Net

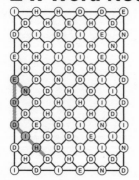

25. Ladies in Waiting

The words are:

- BANJO
- BIGAMY
- COUNTERSUE
- LIVELILY
- OVERJOY
- SALMONELLA
- SUMMARY

26. Debugging Required

They all contain insects:

- Beef: bee
- Blouse: louse
- Dismantle: ant
- Godmother: moth
- Smidgen: midge
- Sniffly: fly

27. Not a Band

The bands are:

- Green Day
- Coldplay
- Queen
- The White Stripes
- The Spice Girls
- The Black Keys
- The Doors
- The Rolling Stones
- Radiohead
- No Doubt

28. Ordered List

Each word contains a number. Placing them in increasing order:

- Homoph<u>one</u>
- Ar<u>two</u>rk
- W<u>eight</u>ed
- Pun<u>ine</u>ss
- At<u>ten</u>tion

29. Four-Letter Words

S I G H
   L O G
   N U B
   Y N C
   O D A
   A I D
   C A R
   E L F

30. A Way with Words

DOG, to form:

- DOGGONE
- DOGHOUSE
- DOGMA
- DOGWOOD

31. Proverb Ally

The proverbs are:

- An Englishman's house is his castle
- If the shoe fits, wear it
- Money isn't everything
- He who laughs last, laughs longest
- If you can't stand the heat, get out of the kitchen
- Crime doesn't pay
- Business before leisure

32. Time for Tea

```
H N V E I A D I M B U U Y G B
P M D A R J E E L E M W E E O
A O I G L I N A A R E N R I G
A H N N M N E L O G G L R A E
D S L A A G E A R U S S I A N
R I E S S A S A M Y E C K E E
M L B R E A K F A S T A G M N
N G U N A H L E E A R R L U R
U N A N A T O O N G I A O N O
Y E I O A R O K O E R V S O O
C O O W L I N E K A A A F C I
T N M A P E G N A R O N Y V B
E O A M I L E J I Y A I E A A
E L H E N I M A H C W R R L C
Y E C N Y E I S A H G Y D A L
```

33. First and Last

- DRUID
- MAXIM
- EDGE
- NEWTON
- LEVEL
- HOOCH
- BEDAUB
- AGENDA
- SATYRS
- KIOSK

34. Another Way with Words

DAY, to form:

- DAYBREAK
- DAYDREAM
- DAYLIGHT
- DAYTIME

35. Number Link

36. Quad Pencil-mark Sudoku

6	4	3	5	1	2	9	7	8
2	5	9	8	6	7	1	4	3
8	1	7	4	9	3	2	6	5
4	3	8	2	5	6	7	1	9
7	6	1	3	8	9	4	5	2
9	2	5	7	4	1	3	8	6
5	8	2	9	7	4	6	3	1
3	7	6	1	2	8	5	9	4
1	9	4	6	3	5	8	2	7

37. Sequel Sequence

The sets of initials are taken from the first published titles of the Harry Potter novels by J K Rowling, listed in chronological order. Each set of initials is the text following '*and the*' in the novel title. Therefore the final entry is D H, since the sequence is:

- Philosopher's Stone
- Chamber of Secrets
- Prisoner of Azkaban
- Goblet of Fire
- Order of the Phoenix
- Half-blood Prince
- Deathly Hallows

38. Worldly Letters

V. They are the initial letters of the planets, working in towards the Sun:

- Neptune
- Uranus
- Saturn
- Jupiter
- Mars
- Earth
- Venus

39. Spiral Crossword

Inward

1-6   POSTAL   7-11   FLOOR

12-19	DRAFTING	35-37	SEC
20-22	NIP	38-42	NADIR
23-28	MUDDLE	43-47	NIGHT
29-31	IFS	48-50	XIS
32-34	ROT		

Outward

50-46	SIXTH	18-16	NIT
45-43	GIN	15-13	FAR
42-40	RID	12-8	DROOL
39-31	ANCESTORS	7-4	FLAT
30-26	FIELD	3-1	SOP
25-19	DUMPING		

40. Parts of a Whole

All of the clues refer to words which contain parts of the body:

- Item of clothing = GARMENT
- Higher place of education = COLLEGE
- Computer = MACHINE
- Very brief unit of time = NANOSECOND
- Decorative light fitting = CHANDELIER
- Wine flavoured with aromatic herbs = VERMOUTH
- Having a golden yellow colour = HONEYED

41. Caesar Salad

These letters have been Caesar-shifted. Shift each letter back three places in the alphabet (so D becomes A, E becomes B, and so on) to reveal some of the ingredients of Caesar salad:

- Lettuce
- Croutons
- Cheese
- Worcestershire Sauce

42. Dice Decision

Labelling the cubes from 1 to 5, left-to-right and top-to-bottom in the order given, the answer is cube 5. Cubes 1 and 2 have their top faces rotated incorrectly, cube 3 has a face that does not appear on the cube net, and cube 4 has its front face rotated incorrectly.

43. Slightly Altered

In each word, the vowels have been shifted backwards by one, so E has become A, I has become E, and so on. Therefore the words are:

- STOCK
- DOWN
- AIR
- CARE
- FIVE
- OUT

All of these words make a phrase when "TAKE" is added in front of them: take stock, take down, take air, take care, take five and take out.

44. Relationship Study

The relationship ends up as **on**, having alternated between on and off throughout the passage:

I felt aband<u>on</u>ed. <u>Off</u>icially she was away for work, but that was merely an illusi<u>on</u>. When I rang her <u>off</u>ice they had not a noti<u>on</u> where she was. She was a serial <u>off</u>ender, of course, for she had d<u>on</u>e all this before.

She brought t<u>off</u>ees with her when she returned. That was a M<u>on</u>day. I was angry, sc<u>off</u>ing at her dish<u>on</u>est <u>off</u>ering.

'You just keep going <u>on</u> at me!' she complained.

I stormed out of the room. When I had cooled <u>off</u> with a c<u>on</u>soling c<u>off</u>ee, I resolved myself and spoke to her.

'H<u>on</u>estly,' I said, 'this could be the last nail in the c<u>off</u>in of our relati<u>on</u>ship'.

45. Multi-gram

- ENLIST
- INLETS
- LISTEN
- SILENT
- TINSEL

46. Shady Challenge

Each line contains a hidden colour, and these are listed in the order of the colours of the rainbow. The missing colour is violet, which should be inserted at the end of the list:

- Hund<u>red</u> dollar bill
- Within radi<u>o range</u>
- When I hurt myself I <u>yell, ow</u>ing to the pain
- Forbidding<u> re-en</u>try
- Rhythm and <u>blues</u>
- Against the wi<u>nd I go</u>
- Shrinking <u>violet</u> (or another suitable phrase)

47. It's All Greek to Me

They are all Greek gods:

- Poseidon
- Hades
- Aphrodite
- Helios
- Ares
- Hypnos
- Aether
- Eros

48. Initial Movies List

- *Butch Cassidy and the Sundance Kid*
- *Eternal Sunshine of the Spotless Mind*
- *Lock, Stock and Two Smoking Barrels*
- *One Flew Over the Cuckoo's Nest*
- *Once Upon a Time in the West*
- *Raiders of the Lost Ark*
- *The Good, the Bad and the Ugly*
- *The Lord of the Rings: The Two Towers*

49. Country Codes

The countries are:

- CHILE (Greek letter 'chi' + LE)
- MONACO (M on ACO)
- PALESTINE (the 'pale' STINE is indicated)
- NORWAY (N or WAY)
- SINGAPORE (SIN ...gap... ORE)
- UGANDA (UG and A)
- UNITED KINGDOM (where the letters are together)
- EAST TIMOR (the Timor on the 'east' side of the page)
- FINLAND (arrows point at the 'fin' and the 'land')

50. Disemvowelled

- BRAD PITT
- GENE KELLY
- JAMES DEAN
- JOHNNY DEPP
- COLIN FIRTH
- TOM HANKS
- MARLON BRANDO
- AL PACINO
- GEORGE CLOONEY

51. Outside Sudoku

9	4	6	8	3	2	1	7	5
5	8	3	7	9	1	2	4	6
2	1	7	4	5	6	8	9	3
1	2	4	3	6	7	5	8	9
3	7	5	9	1	8	6	2	4
8	6	9	2	4	5	3	1	7
6	5	2	1	7	9	4	3	8
4	9	8	5	2	3	7	6	1
7	3	1	6	8	4	9	5	2

52. Hot Stuff

Four of the words – alarm, drill, engine and escape – can be preceded by the word 'fire', and four – breathe, friendly, open and under – can be followed by it.

53. Flavoursome

All of the words anagram to herbs and spices:

- TARRAGON
- CAMOMILE
- MARJORAM
- PARSLEY
- STAR ANISE
- TURMERIC

54. Parking Fine?

INNATE. All of the other words already contain a 'CAR', so there is no room to park, but INNATE does not. Moreover, you could park a car inside INNATE to make INCARNATE.

- PRE<u>CAR</u>IOUS
- MAS<u>CAR</u>PONE
- S<u>CAR</u>LET
- VI<u>CAR</u>
- UN<u>CAR</u>ING
- S<u>CAR</u>Y
- MA<u>CAR</u>ONI

55. Reading Query

All of the words can be pronounced as a series of letters:

- DECAY – D K
- CUTIE – Q T
- OBEDIENCY – O B D N C
- ANEMONE – N M N E

- SEEDY – C D
- ESCAPEE – S K P
- EXCESS – X S

56. Calcudoku

3	2	1	6	4	5	7	8
4	5	8	2	3	7	6	1
2	8	4	3	5	6	1	7
5	6	2	7	8	1	4	3
6	7	5	1	2	8	3	4
7	1	3	8	6	4	2	5
8	3	7	4	1	2	5	6
1	4	6	5	7	3	8	2

57. First Puzzle

All of the words start (thus have a 'first connection') with the same word, CROSS, and each remains a word even when CROSS is removed:

- CROSSROADS
- CROSSWORD
- CROSSFIRE

- CROSSBOW
- CROSSOVER

58. Final Puzzle

All of the words remain a word even when their final letter is removed:

- HEAVE
- QUART
- WEAR
- DIVERS
- CAME
- BADGE
- DAIS

Solutions 2
Diversions

1. Mixed Doubles

The unscrambled words are: TABLE, BOX, HAND, SPEED, HIGH, LONG, ROW, FIGURE, BASKET and LAWN. All of these words appear at the start of names of sports. BOX and ROW are a pair as they both precede -ING. HAND and BASKET are a pair as they both precede -BALL. HIGH and LONG are a pair as they both precede JUMP. SPEED and FIGURE can both precede SKATING. LAWN and TABLE can both precede TENNIS.

2. Five by Five

US Presidents	European Capitals	Spielberg Films	Big Cats	Car Brands
BUSH	ATHENS	BRIDGE OF SPIES	CHEETAH	BMW
FORD	MOSCOW	HOOK	LEOPARD	HONDA
GARFIELD	PARIS	LINCOLN	LION	JAGUAR
HOOVER	RIGA	MINORITY REPORT	PUMA	MINI
TRUMP	ROME	MUNICH	TIGER	TOYOTA

3. Reckoning by the Rules

Rule A is colours of the rainbow, and rule B is colours with six letters. So the completed table should look like this:

Rule A	Rule B	Rules A and B	Neither A nor B
RED	SILVER	ORANGE	PINK
GREEN	PURPLE	YELLOW	GOLD
BLUE	MAROON	VIOLET	AMBER
	COPPER	INDIGO	NAVY
	SALMON		**BLACK**
			WHITE

4. A Sweeping Statement
Mine.

5. Riddle
Lounger, when the letter 'u' is removed.

6. Snake

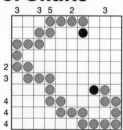

7. A Leading Question
S: it is the first letters of each of the words in the question, taken in ordinary reading order.

8. What's in a Name?
- *Twelfth Night* – the twelfth knight is underlined
- *Much Ado About Nothing* – lots of (i.e. much) 'ado' around a zero (i.e. nothing)
- *Measure for Measure* – a word meaning 'measure', followed by four ('for') measures
- *The Merry Wives of Windsor* – FEW WORD VISIONS is a

'merry' version, i.e. anagram, of WIVES OF WINDSOR
• *A Midsummer Night's Dream* – NIGHTSDREAM is *amid* ('A Mid...') the word SUMMER

9. Jigsaw Box

7	9	3	2	5	1	4	6	8
5	6	8	7	3	4	2	9	1
2	4	1	9	8	6	5	3	7
3	5	2	8	4	9	1	7	6
4	7	6	3	1	5	9	8	2
1	8	9	6	2	7	3	4	5
9	2	4	1	7	8	6	5	3
6	3	7	5	9	2	8	1	4
8	1	5	4	6	3	7	2	9

10. Linked Anagrams Too
The words are:
• FEATURE
• DISH
• HOLDING
• BACK
• MARK

• UNDER
• DEEP
• HOT
• LEVEL
• DOWN

The common theme is WATER, since it can be added as a preceding or following word, or as a prefix or suffix, to all of the words.

11. Number Targets
• 40 = 19 + 21
• 53 = 9 + 21 + 23
• 61 = 7 + 15 + 19 + 20

• 76 = 7 + 9 + 19 + 20 + 21
• 90 = 7 + 19 + 20 + 21 + 23

12. Pyramidal Too
The words are:
• RAT
• DART
• TREAD
• TIRADE
• ASTRIDE
• HARDIEST

• TARNISHED
• DISHEARTEN
• NEARSIGHTED

13. What Ls?

14. Movie Match-Up 2

Alice		*Wonderland*
A Place		*The Sun*
Around the World		*80 Days*
Barefoot		*The Park*
Big Trouble		*Little China*
Death		*Venice*
Down and Out		*Beverly Hills*
Ghost		*The Shell*
Gone		*60 Seconds*
Gorillas	*in*	*The Mist*
How to Lose a Guy		*10 Days*
Last Tango		*Paris*
Lost		*Translation*
Once Upon a Time		*The West*
Pretty		*Pink*
Shakespeare		*Love*
Singin'		*The Rain*
Sleepless		*Seattle*
The Man		*The Iron Mask*
What We Do		*The Shadows*

15. Word Tree
The film is GOOD WILL HUNTING:

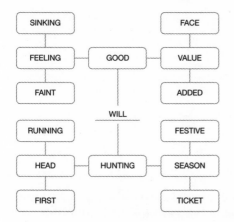

16. A Game of Two Halves

- PEANUT BUTTER and JELLY
- ANTONY and CLEOPATRA
- SIMON and GARFUNKEL
- ABBOTT and COSTELLO
- GILBERT and SULLIVAN
- MACARONI and CHEESE
- ROMEO and JULIET
- STARSKY and HUTCH
- LENNON and MCCARTNEY
- BUTCH CASSIDY and THE SUNDANCE KID
- DR JEKYLL and MR HYDE
- WALLACE and GROMIT

17. Lost in Austen

- ELIZABETH BENNET
- JOHN WILLOUGHBY
- EMMA WOODHOUSE
- FITZWILLIAM DARCY
- GEORGE KNIGHTLEY
- CATHERINE DE BOURGH
- CHARLES BINGLEY
- ELINOR DASHWOOD
- GEORGE WICKHAM
- EDWARD FERRARS

18. Pale Colours

- ROSE
- CORAL
- FUCHSIA
- CARNATION
- PEACH

19. Skyscraper

```
        6   4
    ┌─────────────────┐
    │ 6 │ 1 │ 4 │ 2 │ 5 │ 3 │
  2 │ 5 │ 2 │ 3 │ 4 │ 6 │ 1 │ 2
    │ 4 │ 3 │ 6 │ 5 │ 1 │ 2 │ 3
    │ 2 │ 4 │ 1 │ 6 │ 3 │ 5 │ 2
    │ 3 │ 5 │ 2 │ 1 │ 4 │ 6 │
    │ 1 │ 6 │ 5 │ 3 │ 2 │ 4 │ 3
    └─────────────────┘
        5       2 3
```

20. Platinum Albums

Each of these song titles has had an element from the periodic table replaced by the element that follows immediately after it in the periodic table (i.e. has an atomic number that is one higher). The original song titles are therefore:

- TINY DANCER, by Elton John
- IRONIC, by Alanis Morissette
- NICKELS AND DIMES, by Dolly Parton
- FOLLOW MY LEAD, by Justin Timberlake
- GOLD DIGGER, by Kanye West
- NEON, by John Mayer
- TITANIUM, by David Guetta

21. Secret Ingredients

Each word hides a cooking ingredient:

- Non-ionic
- Unicorn
- Psalter
- Automaton
- Caribbean
- Price

22. Killer Confusion Sudoku

```
┌────────┬────────┬────────┐
│6 4 1│2 5 3│9 8 7│
│9 3 5│7 4 8│6 2 1│
│2 7 8│1 9 6│4 3 5│
├────────┼────────┼────────┤
│7 6 9│3 1 5│2 4 8│
│1 5 3│4 8 2│7 9 6│
│8 2 4│9 6 7│1 5 3│
├────────┼────────┼────────┤
│5 8 7│6 2 4│3 1 9│
│4 9 6│8 3 1│5 7 2│
│3 1 2│5 7 9│8 6 4│
└────────┴────────┴────────┘
```

184

23. Forbidden Planets

- Venus: Why does my o**ven us**ually overcook everything?
- Saturn: The sal**sa turn**ed from red to green.
- Neptune and Earth: The politician was i**nept, une**lectable, and afraid of any nucl**ear th**reat.
- Mars and Uranus: Some Spanish gram**mar s**ounds different in the Hond**uran us**age.

24. Nice and Easy

The words are:

- NEVERTHELESS
- DESCENDED
- EFFERVESCENT
- ELSEWHERE
- CEMETERY
- ESTEEMED
- REFEREE
- EMERGENCY

All of these words contain 'E' as their only vowel.

25. Fruit Bowl

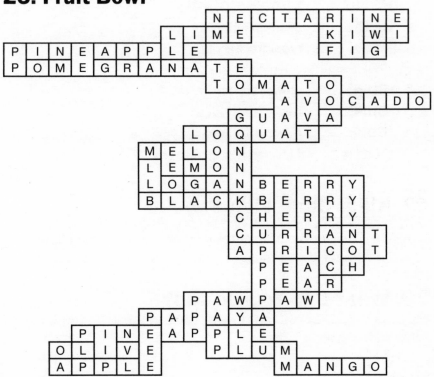

26. Up-front Query

If you delete the first letter of any of the words, you still have a word:

- (C)OVERAGE
- (G)RUMBLE
- (L)AWFUL
- (O)RANGE
- (W)OMEN

27. Word Tour

IRAN	**Tehran's country**
BRAN	edible seed coat
BEAN	legume
BEAM	long piece of timber
TEAM	group working together
TERM	period of tenure
PERM	give hair a wave
PERU	**Lima's country**
PERK	stick up jauntily
PORK	meat from a pig
PORE	opening in the skin
PURE	untainted
CURE	heal
CUBE	power of three
CUBA	**Havana's country**

28. Cinema Conundrum

- *Undercover* is 90 minutes long and is showing at 3pm
- *On The Run* is 120 minutes long and is showing at 6pm
- *Low Profile* is 150 minutes long and is showing at 12pm

29. What Can You Do Too?

These are all things you can run, i.e. you can run a car, run a a race, run a bath and so on.

30. The Second First and Last

- KNACK
- TILT
- YEARLY
- RADAR
- WINNOW
- POLYP
- NEON
- OUZO
- SAGS
- LARVAL
- MAIM

31. Fly Away

They all contain a type of bird:

- Alternate: tern
- Antithesis: tit
- Dovetail: dove
- Knowledge: owl
- Letterhead: rhea
- Probing: robin
- Swanky: swan
- Swiftly: swift

32. Get the Picture

These words pair up to make the titles of one-word Academy Award winning movies: *Braveheart*, *Chicago*, *Moonlight*, *Patton*, *Platoon* and *Spotlight*.

33. Frame Sudoku

	10	17	15	8		22	14		
13	6	2	5	8	1	7	9	4	3
	1	9	4	3	2	6	7	8	5
18	3	7	8	4	5	9	6	2	1	9
8	4	3	1	9	7	8	5	6	2
	2	5	6	1	3	4	8	9	7	24
	7	8	9	2	6	5	1	3	4
	8	6	7	5	4	2	3	1	9	13
16	9	4	3	7	8	1	2	5	6
8	5	1	2	6	9	3	4	7	8	19
	22					6	9	13	

34. Touchy

G	F	H	E	C	A	D	B
E	B	C	F	D	H	G	A
C	G	A	H	E	B	F	D
B	H	F	C	G	D	A	E
F	D	G	B	A	E	H	C
H	A	E	D	F	C	B	G
D	C	B	A	H	G	E	F
A	E	D	G	B	F	C	H

35. Men of Letters

- CADAVER
- CARPETED
- CARJACKING
- CATALANS
- CUSTOMS

- ENVIRONED
- PARLIAMENT
- REMARKED
- RUFFIANS
- SESAME

36. Rain Check

These are all words that can form a two-word phrase with either 'cat' or 'dog' at the start or end. The groups are: ALLEY (CAT), (CAT) BURGLAR, FAT (CAT), (CAT) FLAP and (DOG) DAYS, DIRTY (DOG), HOT (DOG) and (DOG) WHISTLE.

37. Bookending

The completed words are:

- STABLEST
- MEANTIME
- ERASER
- ORATOR
- ESCAPES

- LEGIBLE
- ONION
- ENLIGHTEN
- ICONIC

38. Special Pairs

The words are opposites, where the letters of the second word are found inside the first word, and in the same order.

39. Movie Match-Up

A Room	*A View*
Dances	*Wolves*
Friends	*Benefits*
From Russia	*Love*
Fun	*Dick and Jane*
Gone	*The Wind*
Interview	*A Vampire*
My Dinner	*Andre*
One Night *with*	*The King*
Riding in Cars	*Boys*
Running	*Scissors*
Sleeping	*The Enemy*
The Girl	*The Dragon Tattoo*
The Life Aquatic	*Steve Zissou*
The Man	*The Golden Gun*
They're Playing	*Fire*
Travels	*My Aunt*
Tuesdays	*Morrie*
Waltz	*Bashir*
You Can't Take It	*You*

40. More Newly Named Novels

- *The Age of Innocence*
- *The Sound and the Fury*
- *The Handmaid's Tale*
- *The Big Sleep*
- *The Little Prince*
- *A Room with a View*

41. May Contain Nuts

Each word contains a possible allergen:

- Dimin<u>ut</u>ive
- Boot<u>legg</u>er
- Oa<u>fish</u>ness
- Blow-dr<u>ye</u>r
- B<u>oats</u>wain

42. Proverbial Problem

The proverbs are:

- No good deed goes unpunished

- East is east, and west is west
- Necessity is the mother of invention
- Don't throw the baby out with the bathwater
- Time is a great healer
- The proof of the pudding is in the eating
- Money is the root of all evil

43. Facing Off
The fourth face, with the black triangle.

44. An Odd Scramble
The odd one out is COOL CIDER, since it is an anagram of
CROCODILE, a reptile, while all the others are anagrams of birds.

- CROCODILE
- PENGUIN
- CHICKEN
- ALBATROSS
- FLAMINGO
- PHEASANT
- OYSTERCATCHER
- NIGHTINGALE

45. Spiral Crossword
Inward

1-5	PALMS	28-30	ORE
6-9	APSE	31-35	CIVIL
10-13	ROTS	36-39	EDGE
14-18	ERROR	40-45	PORTER
19-22	RIMS	46-50	LOOPS
23-27	MOODY		

Outward

50-46	SPOOL	26-22	DOOMS
45-41	RETRO	21-16	MIRROR
40-38	PEG	15-9	RESTORE
37-34	DELI	8-4	SPASM
33-27	VICEROY	3-1	LAP

46. Vowel Play
- AER LINGUS
- JAPAN AIRLINES
- ALITALIA
- BRITISH AIRWAYS
- QANTAS
- LUFTHANSA

- EL AL

47. Alternative Puzzle
All of the words consist of two words, perfectly interleaved. In other words, the 'odd' letters make one word, and the other letters make another:
- CALLIOPES = CLIPS and ALOE
- PAINED = PIE and AND
- SCHOOLED = SHOE and COLD
- TRIENNIALLY = TINILY and RENAL

48. Hanjie Sudoku
Each of the numbers in the unshaded region appears twice, except for the number 8 – so 8 is the odd number out.

		9	8	7	1 6	2 5	3 4	4 3	5 2	6 1
	9	9	6	5	7	8	4	3	2	1
	8	4	8	1	6	2	3	9	5	7
	7	2	3	7	1	5	9	4	8	6
1	6	1	9	6	4	7	2	5	3	8
2	5	5	2	8	9	3	1	7	6	4
3	4	3	7	4	8	6	5	1	9	2
4	3	7	4	3	2	9	6	8	1	5
5	2	8	5	2	3	1	7	6	4	9
6	1	6	1	9	5	4	8	2	7	3

49. Clue Connects
All of the answers are anagrams of one another:
- The most computer-obsessed = NERDIEST
- One who lives in a place = RESIDENT
- Added to the middle = INSERTED
- Fashionable people = TRENDIES

50. Five by Five Two

Birds	Roman Gods	Girls names	Planets	Elements
CRANE	VULCAN	SARAH	EARTH	COPPER
SWIFT	DIANA	JANE	MARS	GOLD
KIWI	FLORA	PHOEBE	NEPTUNE	MERCURY
PENGUIN	CERES	ANDREA	SATURN	SILVER
SWALLOW	FAUNA	VIOLA	VENUS	TIN

51. Hide Away

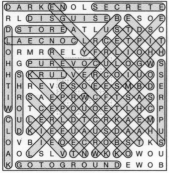

52. Must Dash

The extract contains several 'dot's and 'dash'es:

<u>Do</u>tty <u>do</u>tingly told me an anec<u>dote</u>. It was about a <u>dash</u>ing man in Berm<u>uda sh</u>orts, who had plenty of cash, but his manner was a little slap<u>dash</u>. She said she did not care, but I think the lady <u>do</u>th protest too much – she must need an anti<u>dote</u> for her strong feelings or else she may cross the dreaded <u>dot</u>ted line!

Taken together, these read, on a per-sentence basis, dot dot dot, dash dash dash, dot dot dot, or in other words they represent the urgent alert **SOS** in Morse code, which is often represented with dashes and dots.

53. Winter Clothing

Place an item of winter clothing around the outside of each line ('dress'ing it), to reveal:

- COAT: COLD SWEAT
- MITTEN: MISBEGOTTEN
- HAT: HABIT
- SCARF: SCARE OFF
- GLOVE: GARLIC CLOVE

54. Popular Initials
The combinations are:
- *Bridge Over Troubled Water* by Simon and Garfunkel
- *Dancing Queen* by ABBA
- *Eye Of The Tiger* by Survivor
- *I Heard It Through The Grapevine* by Marvin Gaye
- *I Will Always Love You* by Whitney Houston
- *Rock Around the Clock* by Bill Haley and The Comets
- *Rolling In The Deep* by Adele
- *You're So Vain* by Carly Simon

55. Multi-gram Again
- DEARTHS
- HARDEST
- HATREDS
- THREADS
- TRASHED

56. Vowel Play
- SPEED LIMIT
- MERGE LANES
- ROADWORKS
- GIVE WAY
- DEAD END
- SLOW DOWN
- STEEP INCLINE

57. Further Country Codes
- COSTA RICA (CO star RICA)
- INDIA ('in' DI, A)
- RWANDA (R wand A)
- SLOVENIA (S love NIA)
- SPAIN (S and an indication of pain)
- TOGO (to go drink is indicated)
- HUNGARY (ARY is hung)

58. Timely Sequence

The next number is 0. The sequence is the number of days that each month in the year, from January onwards, is short of 31 days.

59. Sky Movies

All of the titles contain weather-related words:
- *Butch Cassidy and the <u>Sund</u>ance Kid*
- *Gone with the <u>Wind</u>*
- *<u>Hail</u>, Caesar!*
- *<u>Rain</u> Man*
- *<u>Snow</u> White and the Seven Dwarves*

60. Train Timetable

- The 13:15 from platform 2 will get you there in 50 minutes, so you'll arrive at 14:05, which is the earliest possible arrival time
- The 13:30 from platform 1 will get you there in 40 minutes, arriving at 14:10
- The 13:10 from platform 3 will get you there in an hour, and will therefore arrive at 14:10

61. Product Frame Sudoku

2	5	1	6	4	3
4	6	3	5	1	2
1	2	4	3	6	5
5	3	6	4	2	1
6	1	5	2	3	4
3	4	2	1	5	6

Solutions 3
Challenges

1. Capital Stock
They all contain animals:

Ant<u>an</u>anarivo

Ashga<u>bat</u>

At<u>hen</u>s

B<u>rat</u>islava

Bu<u>char</u>est

K<u>har</u>toum

Mos<u>cow</u>

Mus<u>cat</u>

Pa<u>ram</u>aribo

Ra<u>bat</u>

2. Word Tree Too
The film is WEST SIDE STORY:

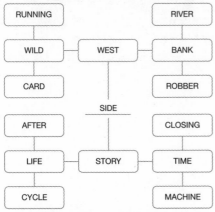

3. Reckoning by the Rules 3
Rule A is countries containing a double letter, and rule B is countries in Europe. So the completed table should look like this:

Rule A	Rule B	Rules A and B	Neither A nor B
SEYCHELLES	CROATIA	GREECE	ECUADOR
CAMEROON	POLAND	ANDORRA	CUBA
PHILIPPINES	DENMARK	RUSSIA	AUSTRALIA
MARSHALL ISLANDS	GERMANY		INDIA
GUINEA-BISSAU	**FRANCE**		**INDONESIA**
MOROCCO			

4. A Pressing Matter
Charge.

5. The Late Shift
The letters of Julius' thought have been shifted forward alphabetically: the first letter by one, the second by two, the third by three, and so on. When this process is reversed, IQPI YOTM becomes HOME TIME.

6. More Number Targets
$28 = 13 + 15$
$40 = 15 + 25$
$55 = 9 + 10 + 11 + 25$

$67 = 9 + 10 + 11 + 13 + 24$
$75 = 11 + 15 + 24 + 25$

7. Hidden Path

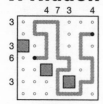

8. Body of Information
The common theme is **parts of the body**. The words should be divided as follows:

Anagrams	Complete the Phrase	Ending With...	Homophones
KEENS (KNEES)	GREEN (FINGERS)	POTATOES (TOES)	FEAT (FEET)
RAMS (ARMS)	SAVING (FACE)	SPLASHES (LASHES)	HARE (HAIR)
SEAR (EARS)	SHAKE (HANDS)	TULIPS (LIPS)	KNOWS (NOSE)
SMUG (GUMS)	SPARE (RIBS)	VERMOUTH (MOUTH)	WASTE (WAIST)

9. Spectator Sports

- Weightlifting (20lb 'lifting' upwards)
- Tennis (ten 'NIS')
- Boxing (a box in 'G')
- Badminton ('TINNOM' is a 'bad' version, or anagram, of 'MINTON')
- Football (a ball that is a foot, i.e. 12 inches, high)

10. Late-breaking Puzzle

All of the words can be split into three words, each of two or more letters, without rearranging their letters:

- ATTENDANCE = AT + TEN + DANCE
- OFTENTIMES = OF + TEN + TIMES
- TOMORROW = TOM + OR + ROW
- TOREADOR = TO + READ + OR

11. Cross Words

12. New World

The anther. These are all anagrams of the capital cities of the countries they were in ('animal'=Manila, 'plaza'=La Paz, 'saunas'=Nassau, 'louse'=Seoul). The capital of Iran is Tehran, which is an anagram of 'anther', a part of a plant.

13. Read Between the Lines

The missing words are: JUDE, JOB, ROMANS, DANIEL, MARK, RUTH, NUMBERS. These are all books of the Bible, so can be arranged in their traditional Biblical order: NUMBERS, RUTH, JOB, DANIEL, MARK, ROMANS, JUDE.

14. Plus This

Ayn. The word in question is 'and': a 'band' is worn on the wrist, a 'hand' is at the end of a wrist, 'land' is solid ground, and 'sand' is at the edge of it (i.e. on the shore). The author is Ayn Rand.

15. Kropki

```
6 1 3 4 5 7 8 2
8 7 4 5 2 6 1 3
7 6 2 8 1 5 3 4
5 3 1 2 4 8 6 7
1 8 6 3 7 2 4 5
3 4 5 7 6 1 2 8
2 5 8 6 3 4 7 1
4 2 7 1 8 3 5 6
```

16. In a Sorry State

THORN ARTS, or any anagram of NORTH STAR. The anagrammed words are:

GOLDEN   GEM
BEAVER   TREASURE
EVERGREEN   PEACE GARDEN

These are US state nicknames, travelling clockwise along the mainland border from California to North Dakota. The next state would be Minnesota, whose nickname is the North Star state.

17. Sounds Familiar

The words defined are: PEA, YOU, ARE, EYE, TEA and WHY. These are all homophones of letters. The corresponding letters, taken in that order, spell out PURITY.

18. Follow the Rule

E2. These letters and numbers refer to the initials and numbers of the kings and queens of Great Britain, in chronological order of their succession to the throne: Anne, George I, George II, George III, George IV, William IV, Victoria, Edward VII, George V, Edward VIII and George VI. The next one is therefore Elizabeth II.

19. Liquid Vowels

- TEQUILA
- ARMAGNAC
- OUZO
- SAMBUCA
- RUM
- ABSINTHE

20. Increasing Sudoku

5	6	7	2	1	8	3	9	4
4	8	1	3	6	9	7	5	2
9	3	2	5	4	7	1	6	8
1	7	4	8	9	3	6	2	5
2	5	8	1	7	6	9	4	3
3	9	6	4	5	2	8	7	1
6	4	3	7	8	5	2	1	9
7	2	5	9	3	1	4	8	6
8	1	9	6	2	4	5	3	7

21. Bridges

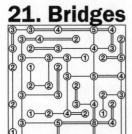

22. Flower Arranging

These are all anagrams of rivers (i.e. 'flow-er's): RHONE (505 miles in length), HUDSON (315 miles), NILE (4,258 miles), LOIRE (629 miles), NIGER (2,597 miles), ARNO (150 miles) and IRTYSH (2,640). The order, based on decreasing lengths of each river, is therefore:

- LINE
- SHIRTY
- REIGN
- ORIEL
- HERON
- HOUNDS
- ROAN

23. Six Notes

Each defines a six-letter word, of which the middle two letters are one of the seven syllables of the do, re, mi musical scale, listed in increasing order:

- UN<u>DO</u>NE
- CA<u>RE</u>ER
- NA<u>MI</u>NG
- SA<u>FA</u>RI
- AB<u>SO</u>RB
- SA<u>LA</u>MI
- SA<u>TI</u>RE

24. Numbers Games

RCELON. These are summer Olympics host cities. The letters removed correspond to the year in which each city hosted the Olympics, based on deleting the 'n'th letter where 'n' is a digit within the year.

- Rio de Janeiro hosted in 2016, so it has had its second (2), first (1) and sixth (6) letters removed
- London hosted in 2012, so it has had its second and first letters removed
- Beijing hosted in 2008, so it has had its second letter removed – there is no eighth letter
- Athens hosted in 2004, so it has had its second and fourth letters removed
- Sydney hosted in 2000, so it has had its second letter removed
- Atlanta hosted in 1996, so it has had its first and sixth letters removed – there is no ninth letter

The host city in 1992 was Barcelona. So, with its first, ninth and second letters removed, the remaining letters spell 'RCELON'.

25. Showing Off
- FRIENDS (the ends of FRI are indicated, i.e. the FRI ends)
- BREAKING BAD ('breaking' written badly, i.e. anagrammed)
- SUITS
- ONCE UPON A TIME (ONCE written upon/over a time)
- THREE'S COMPANY (three S + an abbreviation for COMPANY)

26. The Great Pyramid
The words are as follows:
- ART
- CART
- TRACE
- NECTAR
- RECANTS
- REENACTS
- ENTRANCES
- NECTARINES
- INCINERATES
- INHERITANCES

27. Publication Puzzle
The Billy Bulletin is produced weekly and only read by undergraduates. *The Goat Post* is produced termly and read by all students. *Optima* is produced annually and read by all students and staff.

28. Firsts and Lasts
- AORTA and SORTS
- BUB, DUD, HUH, MUM, NUN, PUP and TUT
- DEAD, REAR, SEAS and TEAT
- BULB, LULL and PULP
- DASHED, RASHER and SASHES
- DEED, PEEP and SEES
- GROG, PROP and TROT

- BIB, DID, GIG, PIP, SIS and TIT
- DOLLED and ROLLER

29. Diagonal Number Link

 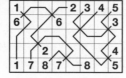

30. Sum Skyscraper

6	3	5	1	4	2
5	1	3	6	2	4
3	4	6	2	1	5
4	6	2	3	5	1
1	2	4	5	6	3
2	5	1	4	3	6

31. Tone Deafness

The anagrammed phrases are:

- SABBATH
- DAY
- FLOYD
- BARRY
- JAMES
- OYSTER CULT
- HOT CHILI PEPPERS

These are 'tone-deaf' in that they are the names of musical artists which have had colours removed from them: Black Sabbath, Green Day, Pink Floyd, Barry White, James Brown, Blue Oyster Cult, Red Hot Chili Peppers.

32. Worldwide Tour

FIJI. This can be deduced most easily by noting that the countries in the list contain every letter of the alphabet except for F, I and J.

33. Salad Days

These are all clues for fruits:

- 'Barrier Boy' clues 'dam son' by synonyms
- 'Woman Stop' clues 'man go' by antonyms
- 'Moose Merry' clues 'gooseberry' by rhyme

- 'Coat Rip' clues 'apricot' by anagram
- 'Lie Chi' clues 'lychee' by homophone

34. What's That?

All of the phrases contain a redundant word:

- Collaborate ~~together~~
- ~~Downward~~ descent
- ~~Exact~~ replica
- ~~First~~ conceived
- ~~Unexpected~~ surprise

35. Facing Off

The fifth face, of the grey square with a nested central white square.

36. Word Search

All of the numbers or numeric words in the entries are replaced with their corresponding digits:

- ACETONE = ACET1
- ADENINE = ADE9
- ANCIENT WORLD = ANCIEN2RLD
- ART WORK = AR2RK
- BREAKS EVEN = BREAK7
- CANINE = CA9
- CLONE = CL1
- CONDITIONER = CONDITI1R
- DOZENTH = 12TH
- ELEVENSES = 11SES
- ENGROSSED = EN144ED
- FEMININE = FEMI9
- FOOTWORK = FOO2RK
- FOURIER = 4IER
- FREIGHT = FR8
- HUNDREDWEIGHT = 100W8
- NON-EXISTENT = 0XIS10T
- OVERWEIGHT = OVERW8
- SUNNINESS = SUN9SS
- SWEET SIXTEEN = SWEET16
- TAKE FIVE = TAKE5
- TENSIONED = 10SI1D
- THOUSANDFOLD = 1000FOLD

- THREE WISE MEN = 3WISEMEN
- UNDERSCORE = UNDER20
- VERMILLION = VER1000000

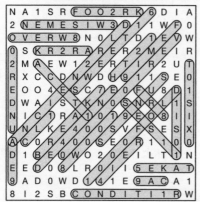

37. Movie Match-Up

All Quiet	The Western Front
Angel	My Shoulder
A Nightmare	Elm Street
Bird	A Wire
Born	The Fourth of July
Breakfast	Pluto
Cat	A Hot Tin Roof
Death	The Nile
Fiddler on	The Roof
Lean	Me
Man	The Moon
Miracle	34th Street
Mutiny	The Bounty
Notes	A Scandal
Snakes	A Plane
Snow Falling	Cedars
Strangers	A Train
The Bridge	The River Kwai
The Greatest Show	Earth
Women	The Verge of a Nervous Breakdown

38. Spiral Crossword

Inward

1-6	BURDEN	26-32	DROWNED
7-10	OPTS	33-37	LOGIC
11-17	OPENING	38-42	OFFER
18-20	NIL	43-50	SCROLLED
21-25	URBAN		

Outward

50-47	DELL	25-23	NAB
46-43	ORCS	22-17	RULING
42-40	REF	16-13	NINE
39-36	FOCI	12-5	POSTPONE
35-30	GOLDEN	4-1	DRUB
29-26	WORD		

39. Characterful Writing

These words and phrases each contain either 'mean' or 'kind', which splits them into two groups:

- **Mean**: Crè**me an**glais, De**mean**our, **Mean**der, Ti**me and** again
- **Kind**: Human**kind**, **Kind**ergarten, Rame**kin d**ish, S**kin-d**eep

40. TV Schedule

- 'A Farm in the City' has run for only one season and has one-hour episodes
- 'Silence is Golden' has run for two seasons and has 40-minute episodes
- 'They Wouldn't Dare' has run for three seasons and has 20-minute episodes

41. One Stair at a Time

To make it one stair at a time, every sentence must take them safely to the next step. And as it happens, they do, for every sentence already *contains* the next 'step':

- Reading the fir**st 'ep**istle' from my sister, now a politician, wasn't easy.
- There was a moment when I thought of throwing it in the wa**ste pa**per basket.

- It was my <u>step</u>brother who finally helped me.
- He made me a mug of hi<u>s tep</u>id tea – a family special.
- The familiar ta<u>ste p</u>romptly cheered me up.
- He told me that his friend, <u>Step</u>hen, had had a similar problem.
- Reading political pamphlets is an acquired ta<u>ste, p</u>erhaps.
- I gave up reading and decided to cut and pa<u>ste p</u>aragraphs to make my own version instead.
- This would be a much better version for her to take door<u>step</u>ping!

So they made it safely to the next floor.

42. A Worthy Puzzle

The words can be grouped based on their contained currencies:
- Hyena, Cayenne and Doyen – yen
- Propounding, Impound and Compound – pound
- Neuron, European and Pleuron – euro

43. Focal Words

All of the words are palindromic:
- LEVEL
- DEIFIED
- MADAM
- STATS
- REDDER
- SOLOS
- PEEP
- ROTOR
- KAYAK

44. Equal Division

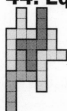

45. TV Introductions

The TV shows are:
- How I Met Your Mother
- Orange is the New Black

- Two and a Half Men
- Sex and the City
- Game of Thrones
- The Big Bang Theory
- The Fresh Prince of Bel-Air

- The Twilight Zone
- Star Trek: The Next Generation
- Buffy the Vampire Slayer

46. A Shark's Tale

They all contain the names of fish:

- The Da Vinci <u>Code</u>
- <u>Shake</u>speare in Love
- A Series of Unfor<u>tuna</u>te Events

- The Amb<u>ass</u>ador
- A <u>Brill</u>iant Young Mind
- Man of St<u>eel</u>

47. Drink Dilemma

- Crocodile's Cool Cider is 5% alcohol and from Australia
- Regal Lager is 4.5% alcohol and from the UK
- Femmefat Ale is 6% alcohol and from Belgium

48. Cheesy Story

This story has a cheesiness quantity of 10, since it contains 10 hidden cheeses:

We were staying in a batt<u>le-dam</u>aged ba<u>roque fort</u>ress for the week. I put on blea<u>ched dark</u> jeans and a ta<u>ffeta</u> blouse and went downstairs to cook an a<u>pricot ta</u>rt. I began by putting fruit in a <u>pan.</u> <u>Eeri</u>ly, the cooking pots were clattering. It made the pan<u>s tilt one</u> way and then the other, here in <u>Monterey. Jack</u>, my partner, heard nothing and dismissed my fears. He called th<u>em mental</u> images, and my ordinary <u>par. Me, sane</u>?!

49. Number Darts

The totals can be formed like this, working outwards from the centre for each sum:

- 82 = 29 + 15 + 25 + 13
- 83 = 37 + 26 + 8 + 12
- 118 = 34 + 39 + 32 + 13

50. Wet Room

Each of the entries clues a word or phrase containing the letters sequence HHO, or in other words H_2O – i.e. water:

- Withhold
- Coach house
- Youth hostel
- Fish hook
- Roughhousing
- British Honduras

51. Aesthetic Connection

When pronounced, all of the words contain a silent letter.

52. One Direction

South. The other words contain north, east and south:

- U<u>NORTH</u>ODOX
- BE<u>AST</u>LY
- A<u>WEST</u>RUCK

53. One Connection

They all contain three consecutive letters that are also consecutive in the alphabet:

- OVE<u>RST</u>OCK
- <u>DEF</u>ACE
- SOM<u>NO</u>LENCE
- <u>STU</u>BBORN
- HYDRO<u>XYZ</u>INE
- E<u>CDE</u>MIC

Solutions 4
Enigmas

1. Mixed Signals

The code word is CHUCKLED. The words of your message are misheard NATO alphabet words. The message you should have received is: CHARLIE HOTEL UNIFORM CHARLIE KILO LIMA ECHO DELTA, spelling out the code word CHUCKLED.

2. Take It Up a Notch

The right-hand column contains definitions of the words defined in the left-hand column after they have had 'up' added to them. The pairs are:

Bestow: GIVE	Surrender: GIVE UP
Choose: PICK	Collect: PICK UP
Circle: RING	Call by phone: RING UP
Create: MAKE	Reconcile: MAKE UP
Cut shorter: CROP	Appear: CROP UP
Draw into the mouth: SUCK	Be obsequious: SUCK UP
Exhale rapidly: BLOW	Explode: BLOW UP
Fissure: CRACK	Start laughing: CRACK UP
Grab: SEIZE	Become immobile: SEIZE UP
Perform a role: ACT	Misbehave: ACT UP
Possess: OWN	Confess: OWN UP
Project: THROW	Regurgitate: THROW UP
Rear: BACK	Reverse: BACK UP
Rears: BOTTOMS	Cheers: BOTTOMS UP
Receive: GET	Rise: GET UP

Rest: BREAK

Shellfish: CLAM

Shout in support: CHEER

Tube: PIPE

Water source: WELL

Separate: BREAK UP

Stop talking: CLAM UP

Become happier: CHEER UP

Speak out: PIPE UP

Begin to cry: WELL UP

3. State of the Art

The completed words are:

- **AL**C**OH**OL
- A**SC**ERTAI**NM**ENT
- **CA**TERPI**L**LAR
- FO**R**BID**D**ING
- H**AZAR**DOUS

- **MO**NO**GA**MOUS
- PRE**VA**LE**NC**E
- SI**NE**W**Y**
- WIG**WAMS**

The missing letters are two-letter US state abbreviations. When the corresponding states are shaded on the map, the result (along with the two states that are already shaded) is:

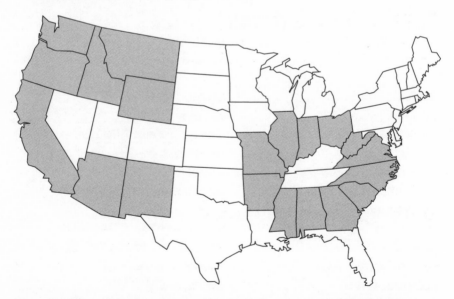

The shaded states visually spell out the letters CO, which is the state abbreviation for Colorado. Therefore Colorado is the answer.

4. Period Drama

KEROUAC = 276. The numbers are obtained by breaking down each name into symbols of chemical elements, as hinted at by the word 'Period' in the title:

- Au S Te N
- Br O N Te
- H Ar Dy
- La W Re N Ce
- S Te In Be C K / S Te I N Be C K
- K Er O U Ac

The atomic numbers of the component elements are then added to provide the final total.

5. Arithmetic for Vexillologists

The missing value is 8. Each line is a sum that uses the flags of the mentioned countries. The central flag in each row is to be read as either a + or a × sign, while the other two countries represent numbers.

- Lithuania has three stripes, so represents 3. Switzerland represents a + sign, and Poland has two stripes. Therefore the first line reads 3 + 2 = 5.
- Nigeria has three stripes, Jamaica has a diagonal cross, and Guinea has three stripes, giving 3 × 3 = 9.
- Canada has three stripes, Dominica has a plus, and Barbados has three stripes, giving 3 + 3 = 6.
- Thailand has five stripes, Georgia has a plus, and Tajikistan has three stripes, giving 5 + 3 = 8.

6. Wraparound Sudoku

9	5	1	3	4	7	6	8	2
4	6	8	1	7	3	2	9	5
5	8	3	9	2	4	7	6	1
2	9	5	4	8	1	3	7	6
8	2	6	7	5	9	4	1	3
7	4	2	8	3	6	1	5	9
6	7	4	5	1	2	9	3	8
3	1	9	2	6	5	8	4	7
1	3	7	6	9	8	5	2	4

7. Roman Emperors

5. The number is the sum of the Roman numerals contained in each name: **CL**au**DI**us = 651, Ga**L**ba = 50, **VI**te**LLI**us = 107, **TI**tus = 1, **DoMI**t**I**an = 1502, and Ner**V**a = 5.

8. Common Bond

TLD. These are the intials of Bond films in reverse order: *Spectre, Skyfall, Quantum of Solace, Casino Royale, Die Another Day, The World Is Not Enough, Tomorrow Never Dies, GoldenEye* and *Licence to Kill.* The previous one is *The Living Daylights.*

9. Novel Presentations

- *The Catcher in the Rye* (THE CATCHER inside THE RYE)
- *Little Women*
- *Brave New World* (BRAVE + new (anagrammed) WORLD)
- *Middlemarch*
- *Oliver Twist*
- *Fahrenheit 451*
- *On the Road* (ROAD on top of, or 'on', THE)
- *Three Men in a Boat* (three lots of MEN inside BOAT)
- *The Big Snooze*
- *Atonement* (an 'AT' symbol on 'EMENT')

10. Not Needed

An extra letter has been added to each word when it has been placed in the grid. Taken in the order of the clues as given, these extra letters spell out EXTRA LETTERS, the answer.

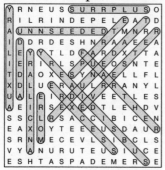

11. Daily Presenting

Alan Partridge. Each two-word phrase contains a word from one of the twelve days of Christmas, counting down from 'swans a-swimming'.

12. Medals Table

The completed table should look like this:

Sport	G	S	B
Artistic Gymnastics	1	3	0
Basketball	0	1	2
Dressage	1	2	0
Greco-Roman Wrestling	2	1	0
Swimming	1	1	0
Weightlifting	2	0	0

'G' is how many 'g's there are in the sport's name, 'S' is how many 's's there are, and 'B' is how many 'b's there are.

13. Increasing Complexity

The words form a word pyramid, i.e. each solution adds a letter to the letters found in the previous word:

- CAT
- CANT
- ENACT
- TRANCE
- CERTAIN
- INTERACT
- INTRICATE
- RECITATION
- INTERACTION
- INDOCTRINATE

14. Nothing in Common?

None of them have any letters in common with their country:

- Cairo, Egypt
- Lima, Peru
- Montevideo, Uruguay
- Rome, Italy
- Suva, Fiji
- Tokyo, Japan

- Vaduz, Liechtenstein

15. Heirs and Graces

These words are anagrams of Shakespearean characters:

- Cordelia
- Goneril
- Regan
- Ophelia

- Miranda
- Edgar
- Portia
- Desdemona

While seven of the names refer to Shakespearean daughters, Edgar is a Shakespearean son – so his name is the odd one out, and therefore 'Raged' is the odd word out.

16. Don't Look!

Touch. The grid containing circles is split into five 2×3 rectangles, each of which represents a Braille letter. These letters, from left-to-right, read T O U C H.

17. What am I?

I am the word 'let':

- Scar + let = red
- Trip + let = one of three babies
- Ham + let = Shakespearean prince

- Let + ter = a character
- Permit = let
- To rent = let

18. Dashing Around

Sideways. Each line of the question represents a letter in Morse code: a one-syllable word represents a dot and a two-syllable word represents a dash. This gives: dot dot dot/ dot dot/ dash dot dot/ dot/ dot dash dash/ dot dash/ dash dot dash dash/ dot dot dot. This spells out 'SIDEWAYS' in Morse code, which is also an answer to the question 'which way up?'

19. Doubling Down

The dodo. Each word contains two occurences of one of the seven syllables of the do re mi scale. The one syllable not featured is 'do', which appears twice in 'dodo'.

20. Off the Rails

It's at Oxford Circus. The message is written in a rail fence cipher on two rails, which means that the message has been encoded by writing the letters in a zig-zag line bouncing up and down from top-to-bottom and bottom-to-top as you read from left-to-right. In other words, reading left-to-right, the message was encoded by writing it like this:

I		S		T		X		O		D		I		C		S
	T		A		O		F		R		C		R		U	

...and then the encoded message was created by taking the letters from the first row followed by the letters from the second row.

21. Making Waves

The sailor could communicate using semaphore, waving his arms around ('Making Waves') with flags. The year of each battle can be treated as a time on a clock, so for example The Battle of Trnava, which took place in 1430, could be considered to be 14:30. Holding flags in the time for 2:30 on an analogue clock makes the semaphore symbol for 'E'. The full set of battle dates will spell out, in semaphore, the word ENIGMA: 1430 (2:30 – E), 1640 (4:40 – N), 1950 (7:50 – I), 1825 (6:25 – G), 1915 (7:15 – M) and 1930 (7:30 – A).

22. Triple Triplets

The clues solve to triplets of words whose central letters are all identical. In addition, all nine words start with the same letter that they end with *and* in all three sets those three letters are D, R and S:

- DASHED, RASHER, SASHES
- DINGED, RINGER, SINGES
- DEAD, REAR, SEAS

23. Movie Match-Up

A Fistful		Dollars
A History		Violence
Anatomy		A Murder
Bridge		Spies
Children		Men
City		God
Dawn		The Dead
Eternal Sunshine		The Spotless Mind
Invasion		The Body Snatchers
Lawrence	of	Arabia
Little Shop		Horrors
Out		Africa
The Best Years		Our Lives
The Bride		Frankenstein
The Grapes		Wrath
The Lives		Others
The Silence		The Lambs
The Sound		Music
The Treasure		The Sierra Madre
The Wizard		Oz

24. Dice Decision

Labelling the cubes from 1 to 5, in the order given from left-to-right and then top-to-bottom, the answer is cube 4.

Cube 1 has its front and top faces swapped; cube 2 has its side face rotated incorrectly; cube 3 has its top face rotated incorrectly; cube 5 has its top and side faces swapped.

25. Grey Matter

Each of these song titles has been altered so that the name of one shade of grey is replaced with a different shade of grey.

The titles should be:
- *Smoke on the Water* by Deep Purple
- *When Doves Cry* by Prince
- *Maxwell's Silver Hammer* by The Beatles
- *Bennie and the Jets* by Elton John

26. Enlightened

All of the sentences, apart from one, contain a source of light. Therefore the darkest sentence is 'But then, she saw him enter the garden.', which contains no light at all:

In spite of lamentable circumstances, she kept on going – gardening kept her calm. But she felt so misunderstood by him. It was flight or fight. She clenched her fists and clamped her lips shut.

But then, she saw him enter the garden.

She seized some soil from a nearby planter; next, she threw it at him. Her heart was ablaze! She took his precious, fragrant orchids and she ripped them to shreds, right in front of his eyes. She was full of fire.

27. Flying Friends

All of the birds are flying in the grid, i.e. drawn in the shape of a bird in flight.

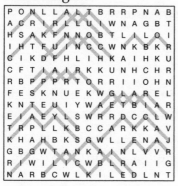

28. Holed Calcudoku

¹²⁺3	2	⁴⁸ˣ8	⁶ˣ6	²⁴ˣ1	¹⁴⁰ˣ7	5	4
7	²⁸⁰ˣ5	6	1	2	3	4	⁸⁻8
⁶⁰ˣ5	7	²⁴ˣ3	8	4	1	⁶6	2
6	8	1	2	5	4	7	¹⁸ˣ3
2	⁹⁶ˣ6	4	7	8	5	¹³⁺3	1
⁵⁺1	4	7	5	3	8	2	6
4	1	5	3	⁴²ˣ6	⁸⁺2	8	⁷⁻7
⁴⁸ˣ8	3	2	4	7	6	1	5

29. Feeling Tense

Each word conceals a word which can be paired with another concealed word to form the same verb in both the past and present tenses:

- After<u>shave</u> and Eye<u>shadow</u>
- Ani<u>seed</u> and Chain<u>saw</u>
- A<u>shine</u>ss and Di<u>shone</u>st
- C<u>run</u>ch and T<u>ran</u>sport
- Cultiv<u>ate</u> and Me<u>atb</u>all

30. Novel Introductions

The novels are:

- *One Hundred Years of Solitude* by Gabriel Garcia Marquez
- *The Bell Jar* by Sylvia Plath
- *The Count of Monte Cristo* by Alexandre Dumas
- *The Color Purple* by Alice Walker
- *To Kill a Mockingbird* by Harper Lee
- *The Picture of Dorian Gray* by Oscar Wilde

31. Written Problem

All of the words can be written on just the middle row of a QWERTY keyboard:

- SALADS
- FLASKS
- FLAGS
- FLASH
- GLASS
- ASHFALL
- ALASKA

32. Connection Question

The words form pairs of anagrams of one another:

- COUNTRIES and NEUROTICS
- TRIANGLES and GNARLIEST
- RESIDENTS and TIREDNESS
- GREATNESS and SERGEANTS
- EMIGRANTS and STREAMING

33. More Number Darts

The totals can be formed like this, working outwards from the centre for each sum:

- 50 = 27 + 11 + 12
- 64 = 35 + 17 + 12

- $66 = 8 + 37 + 21$
- $98 = 29 + 31 + 38$

34. Add Homonym

- All in – awl inn
- Sore spot – saw spot
- Top floor – top flaw
- Bear arms – bare alms
- Sealing wax – ceiling whacks
- Throne room – thrown rheum

35. Back and Forth

All of the words can sometimes be their own opposite:

- SANCTION – to approve, or to disallow
- OVERSIGHT – a watching-over process, or a failure to see
- BOUND – tied down, or a leap up
- DUST – to add dust, or to remove dust
- LEFT – remained, or went away
- RESIGN – give up, or sign up again
- SCREEN – show, or conceal
- TRANSPARENT – obvious, or impossible to see
- TEMPER – Soften (as in language), or harden (as in steel)

36. Equal Division

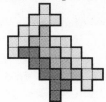

37. Word Twins

These are all the surnames of well-known actors. They pair up based on having the same first name:

- Tom Cruise and Tom Hardy
- Michael (J.) Fox and Michael Sheen
- Stephen Fry and Stephen Merchant
- Chris Pine and Chris Rock

38. Elemental Chemicals

All of the elements can be written using just element symbols from the Periodic Table. There are multiple ways of writing some words, but possibilities include:

- Phosphorus – P H O S P H O Ru S
- Silicon – S I Li Co N
- Iron – Ir O N
- Tin – Ti N
- Arsenic – Ar Se Ni C
- Bismuth – B I Sm U Th
- Xenon – Xe N O N
- Neon – Ne O N

39. Just a Second

Each sequence consists of the second letters of words in a common sequence, so the answers are:

- E: ONE, TWO, THREE, FOUR, FIVE, SIX, SEVEN
- U: JANUARY, FEBRUARY, MARCH, APRIL, MAY, JUNE, JULY
- U: MONDAY, TUESDAY, WEDNESDAY, THURSDAY, FRIDAY, SATURDAY, SUNDAY
- I: RED, ORANGE, YELLOW, GREEN, BLUE, INDIGO, VIOLET

40. Double Negatives

I am not feeling positive, because the aggregate result of all the hidden 'nots' in the passage is an overall 'not'. Double negatives usually creative a positive, but adding in another negative creates a negative again. An even number of 'not's creates a positive, while an odd number of 'not's creates a negative. Overall there are 19 'not's, so the result is negative:

'Another year, another me,' I said to myself. 'And this year I'm not going to make the same mistakes as last year.'

I began to annotate my notebooks from the previous year. At first, the task was quite hypnotic. After a while, however, knots began to form in my stomach, which always denotes trouble.

Every year has become so monotonous. Notionally, I'm changing, but I now see it is <u>not</u> really the case. There's no dom<u>ino</u> theory here.

I poured myself a glass of Pi<u>not</u> and let my belt out a <u>not</u>ch. I had barely <u>not</u>iced the year passing. My <u>not</u>oriety had increased, but what had I really gained?

'A<u>not</u>her year, a<u>not</u>her me,' I said to myself. 'Or <u>not</u>!'

41. Common Parts
They all define a verb which is a homonym for a part of the body:
- Stomach
- Foot
- Hand
- Arm
- Rib
- Eye

42. Double Concealment
Each word contains a hidden word, which itself then forms a pair with another entry when combined with 'and':
- <u>Bat</u>ches and <u>Ball</u>et
- C<u>left</u> and F<u>right</u>en
- Cl<u>ock</u> and Jock<u>ey</u>
- Imp<u>eaches</u> and S<u>cream</u>ing
- Min<u>ute</u> and Thunder<u>bolt</u>
- Sel<u>fish</u> and Wood<u>chips</u>

43. Blod Broothers
The pairs are:

Blud – blood	Foon – fun
Boughin – boffin	Coff – cough
Deight – date	Frate – freight
Feald – field	Miel – meal
Feand – fiend	Miet – meat
Ligher – liar	Hiar – higher
Mude – mood	Crood – crude
Pough – puff	Tuff – tough
Poughst – post	Tho – though
Tiot – shut	Acshun – action

44. Foreign Films
The country at the end of each movie title has been replaced by an anagram of that country's capital city. The original titles are:

- *A Passage to India* (New Delhi)
- *Big Trouble in Little China* (Beijing)
- *Good Morning, Vietnam* (Hanoi)
- *The Boys from Brazil* (Brasilia)
- *The Prince of Egypt* (Cairo)

45. Minesweeper Message

The hidden message somewhat prosaically reads 'THE ANSWER':

46. Word Report

These are definitions of heteronyms, i.e. words which are spelled the same but pronounced differently. They are:

- Attribute: To regard as belonging to; property or quality
- Conduct: Transmit heat; manner of behaviour
- Contest: Call into question; competition
- Contract: Become narrower; formal agreement
- Excuse: Forgive; explanation of behaviour
- Object: Tangible thing; make a complaint
- Permit: Official certificate; allow
- Project: Proposal; throw forwards
- Refuse: Decline; waste

47. Wrap-around Number Link

48. In and Out

The answers form two word pyramids, joined at the shortest word – or a word 'hourglass', more pictorially. Specifically, each solution from the top half of the clues contains the same letters as the word before it, but with one fewer letter; and each solution from the bottom half of the clues contains the same letters as the word before it, but with one extra letter.

- COMEDOWNS
- WOODSMEN
- SWOONED
- ENDOWS
- SOWED
- WOES
- OWE
- WORE
- WORSE
- SHOWER
- SHOWIER
- WORTHIES
- OTHERWISE

49. Take It Away

The word 'SUPER' (which can mean 'great') can be removed from the solution words clued by all of the phrases, while still in each case leaving behind a valid English word:

- SUPERIMPOSED
- SUPERSTORE
- SUPERSTAR
- SUPERVISOR

50. Cryptic Connection

They are all signs of the Zodiac:

- Scorpio – score + p + owe
- Aquarius – aqua + re + us
- Pisces – pi + sees

51. Friendly Names

The names pair up so that a country's name can be read across the join between the end of one name and the start of the other. The exception is CHAD, which is already a country by itself:

- Armenia: CARMEN / IAN
- Canada: DUNCAN / ADAM
- Chad: CHAD
- Chile: MITCH / ILENE
- Ghana: LEIGH / ANASTASIA
- Iran: ALASTAIR / ANNABEL
- Japan: SONJA / PANSY
- Kenya: KEN / YASMINE
- Laos: ANGELA / OSBORNE
- Yemen: SKYE / MENA

52. Double Down

Each clue refers to two words, each of which is spelt identically other than that the second of the two words has a double letter replaced with a single letter. These eliminated letters then spell out 'ALMOST DONE'.

- A: NAAN / NAN
- L: BELL / BEL
- M: COMMA / COMA
- O: GOOD / GOD
- S: FUSSED / FUSED
- T: BITTER / BITER
- D: BIDDING / BIDING
- O: ROOT / ROT
- N: PLANNED / PLANED
- E: WEED / WED

53. Final Bite

The grid is a 'hanjie' puzzle, as seen in puzzle 48 of chapter 2. Solve the hanjie to reveal the image shown to the right.

Each line now represents either a letter, or (if a solidly filled line) a gap between words. The puzzle has 'bite' in the title, which is a homophone for 'byte', suggesting a code that a computer might use. Further, the question asks you to reveal every 'bit', which indicates that you should consider each square as a binary bit – i.e. a binary digit. The message therefore reads, with decimal equivalents shown in brackets: 10100 (20), 01000 (8), 00101 (5), gap, 01100 (12), 00001 (1), 10011 (19), 10100 (20), gap, 00101 (5), 01110 (14), 01001 (9), 00111 (7), 01101 (13), 00001 (1).

These numbers can be converted to letters on the basis of A=1, B=2, C=3 and so on, to read: THE LAST ENIGMA.

Which it, indeed, is.